10
Ten Steps Ahead

What
Separates
Successful
Business
Visionaries
from
the
Rest
of
Us

10

Ten
Steps
Ahead

ERIK CALONIUS

PORTFOLIO / PENGUIN

PORTFOLIO / PENGUIN
Published by the Penguin Group
Penguin Group (USA) Inc., 375 Hudson Street,
New York, New York 10014, U.S.A.
Penguin Group (Canada), 90 Eglinton Avenue East, Suite 700,
Toronto, Ontario, Canada M4P 2Y3
(a division of Pearson Penguin Canada Inc.)
Penguin Books Ltd, 80 Strand, London WC2R 0RL, England
Penguin Ireland, 25 St. Stephen's Green, Dublin 2, Ireland
(a division of Penguin Books Ltd)
Penguin Books Australia Ltd, 250 Camberwell Road, Camberwell,
Victoria 3124, Australia
(a division of Pearson Australia Group Pty Ltd)
Penguin Books India Pvt Ltd, 11 Community Centre, Panchsheel Park,
New Delhi – 110 017, India
Penguin Group (NZ), 67 Apollo Drive, Rosedale, Auckland 0632,
New Zealand (a division of Pearson New Zealand Ltd)
Penguin Books (South Africa) (Pty) Ltd, 24 Sturdee Avenue,
Rosebank, Johannesburg 2196, South Africa

Penguin Books Ltd, Registered Offices:
80 Strand, London WC2R 0RL, England

First published in 2011 by Portfolio / Penguin,
a member of Penguin Group (USA) Inc.

1   3   5   7   9   10   8   6   4   2

Copyright © Erik Calonius, 2011
All rights reserved

Grateful acknowledgment is made for permission to reprint an excerpt from *Glengarry Glen Ross* by
David Mamet. Copyright © 1982, 1983 by David Mamet.
Used by permission of Grove / Atlantic, Inc.
The figure on page 155 is reprinted with permission from L.A. Adamic and N. Glance, "The Political
Blogosphere and the 2004 U.S. Election: Divided They Blog," *Proceedings of the 3rd International
Workshop on Link Discovery,* NY: Association for Computing Machinery, 2005:37

ISBN 978-1-59184-376-4

Printed in the United States of America
Set in Garamond 3
Designed by Elyse Strongin

To Nancy and Michelle,
and especially for my Eagle Scout, Matthew

CONTENTS

Ten 10 Steps Ahead

INTRODUCTION

In 1994, Virgin Group CEO Richard Branson had good reason to pop the cork on the bubbly: He had sold Virgin Music to EMI Group for a billion dollars. And just as sweet, he had won a nasty legal battle against British Airways. Now, Virgin Atlantic—the airline he had founded in 1984 with a single, leased Boeing 747—was poised to expand its service throughout the world. But while his friends and colleagues were celebrating, Branson was already looking ahead. Airline travel was only the beginning, he mused. Space travel couldn't be far behind. He was so certain of this that he had registered a trademark for Virgin *Galactic* Airways.

"You must be joking!" Branson recalls people telling him. "Okay," Branson replied with a grin, "then Virgin *Intergalactic* Airways!"[1] His friends just shook their heads.

But they should have known better by then. For the last 30 years, Branson has had an uncanny ability to see where the world is heading—or, more accurately, the uncanny ability to *shape* where the world is heading. His bold moves have taken Virgin from record sales to recording stars; from Virgin Atlantic Airlines to Virgin Trains; from Virgin health clubs to Virgin Insurance and, most recently, to Virgin Hotels, a new chain of luxury digs.

And now—wouldn't you know it—Virgin is going into space. The Virgin craft, a six-passenger spaceship named *SpaceShipTwo,* is being readied for its launch in 2012 from Virgin's own spaceport in New Mexico. The price of a ticket: $200,000. For that, you get to ride 60 miles into the edge of space; unbuckle your seat belt and float around; and, on the descent, take a gander through *SpaceShipTwo's* oversized porthole windows at the glories of Mother Earth below. In its first year of operation, says Branson, Virgin Galactic will put more people into space than have been there since the beginning of space travel in 1961 (that's slightly more than 500). In fact, there's a waiting list already.[2]

By anyone's definition, Branson is a visionary. He sees what is up ahead and acts accordingly. And he's not alone. Right now, someone somewhere is peering into the future. Perhaps they're in their proverbial garage workshop. Or in a corporate cubicle. Or on a retail floor. But wherever they are, they are seeing something that the rest of us are missing. Maybe it's a trend, or a technology, or a business model. Whatever it is, they are making their plans, searching for money, trying to convert skeptics into believers.

As a reporter and foreign correspondent for the *Wall Street Journal,* as Miami bureau chief for *Newsweek,* and as a writer for *Fortune* magazine, I've had for the last twenty-five years the opportunity to rub shoulders with some of the nation's most visionary business entrepreneurs. What's it like hanging around with a Richard Branson or a Steve Jobs? The word I might use is awesome— not in the colloquial sense but in the sense that at some point you find yourself peering over at them and wondering (with a certain amount of awe) how in the world they've accomplished what they have. Sure they're human, but the arc of their success—and particularly the vision that has put them so far ahead of everyone else—is sometimes hard to comprehend.

How, for instance, did Steve Jobs turn his exile from Apple in 1985 into a triumphant return 13 years later, one that gave the world iMacs, iPhones, and iPads? How has Richard Branson jumped from record seller to record maker to airline owner to insurance man and on and on . . . making the building of a billion-dollar empire look easy? What mix of luck, talent, and vision gave Berry Gordy Jr. the stuff to build Motown, or—on the West Coast—Andy Grove to build Intel? How, in other words, did they get ten steps ahead of the rest of us? Where does this gift called vision come from?

Those questions have been asked many times over the years. But a new source of answers has only recently arisen. Frankly, I wasn't aware of it myself. But while working with Dan Ariely on *Predictably Irrational,* I was introduced to the works of Daniel Kahneman and Amos Tversky, and the new world of cognitive psychology. Following that, a book with brain scientist and Internet entrepreneur Jeff Stibel (*Wired for Thought: How the Brain Is Shaping the Future of the Internet*) introduced me to Eric Kandel, Antonio Damasio, Reed Montague, and other pioneers in brain science. Since collaborating on those books, I've come to realize that a scientific revolution is under way, one that includes new discoveries by an array of neuroscientists, physicists, biologists, psychologists, psychiatrists, and even philosphers. It's all about the brain; in the last 20 years we have learned more about the biology of the brain and how it shapes our behavior than has been known since the beginning of history.

In particular, scientists are discovering that the brain is a *visionary* device—that its primary function is to create *pictures* in our minds that can be used as blueprints for things that do not yet exist. They are also learning that our brains can work *subconsciously* to solve problems that we cannot crack through conscious reasoning, and that the brain is a relentless pattern seeker, constantly reinventing the world.

We now see how certain neurotransmitters, like dopamine, can drive us to pursue our dreams and how others, like serotonin, can nourish our emotional skills so that others will take up our cause. We are realizing that the brain is always learning and changing; that very little is fixed or predetermined; that the brain is capable of providing us with more insight into ourselves and the world than we've ever realized before.

We now have a new understanding of what makes a visionary, and a new lens with which to examine the visionary's life. In the ensuing chapters, then, I will wield that lens to show you how visionaries awaken to ideas, and how they use their powers of visualization to move objects and ideas around in their mind's eye until they stumble on a perspective that cracks the opportunity wide open.

We will see the importance of *intuition* to visionaries—and how they must use it carefully. We will learn how *courage* is the element that separates visionaries from mere dreamers, how visionaries are willing to get out and fight for their dreams. And we will see how *emotional intelligence* is part of the visionary makeup, how visionaries must have the chemistry and charisma to attract supporters for their dreams, building allies and networks so that the dreams will thrive. And then there is *luck*. None of the visionaries in this book could have succeeded without luck—in finding the right idea, in finding the right people. So where does their luck come from?

I haven't written about political, religious, or artistic visionaries in this book. I've focused on business visionaries, entrepreneurs who conceive a product or business and then see it through over years, even decades, to success. I've had the opportunity to meet or at least talk with all the visionaries mentioned in the book (with the notable exception of Walt Disney). These are people whose power and presence I have felt firsthand.

It's an unusual undertaking, connecting the mystery of the visionary to the new developments in brain science. But the most interesting insights often arise from an intersection of ideas, and I hope it is true in this case too. In the pages ahead you will find some surprises, I believe, and some illuminating insights as well.

CHAPTER ONE

The Elements of Vision

I clearly remember the morning when Steve Jobs and I met at the garage in Los Altos, California, where he started Apple Computer. I arrived at the modest ranch-style house a bit early and rang the doorbell. His mother answered and graciously showed me around while we waited for Steve.

There were quite a few pictures on the walls of Jobs in his earlier days. Lots of flowers in the hair, flowing white robes, bare feet, and incense. I had the feeling that he would have been flummoxed and a bit embarrassed had he known his mother was encouraging me to peer into his past. After all, he was no longer Steve of the flowing white robes, but Steve of the black turtleneck and worn blue jeans.

I went back outside. Jobs arrived in his black Mercedes a few minutes later, and sat in the car for several minutes speaking animatedly over his car phone. I could hear the words "Pixar" through the partly opened window, which made no impression on me. That stunning success was still ahead.

When he emerged, we chatted briefly. He went into the house to greet his mother. Then he came out, and we lifted the garage door.

The place was mostly empty, but what struck me first was the calendar on the wall. It depicted all the U.S. presidents, from George Washington onward. The "current" president, according to the yellowed calendar (circa 1977), was none other than Jimmy Carter.

As Jobs looked around, I could see the transformation in his face. "This is where I sat," he said, pointing to one corner of the garage. His eyes grew slightly wider. "And Woz's place was over here," he said, pointing to the spot where his partner Steve Wozniak had worked. Jobs stood there looking at nothing, yet I could feel the garage returning to what it was in 1976, with young Jobs and Wozniak, and a few friends, assembling Apple computers and packing them into boxes. "That was the entire shipping department," he said with a laugh, focusing his eyes on the slab of concrete at the front of the garage. "The table was right there."[1]

We turned from the inside of the garage and looked out over the neighborhood. Jobs told me how he used to bicycle around the streets with his friends. The garage doors in the neighborhood were always open, particularly on Saturdays, he said, and the kids would stop by to watch what the neighborhood fathers—most of them engineers in the nearby electronics industry—were building in their spare time. Considering the technology revolution that had transpired within a few miles of the Jobs home—with the invention of the vacuum tube, the electronic oscillator, the semiconductor, and much more over the years—there was a lot of stuff in the garages for Jobs and his friends to ogle. That proximity to the world of electronics—combined with a HeathKit electronics kit that a neighbor gave him—had set Jobs on his way.

Sweeping his gaze over his old neighborhood, Jobs fell silent. One could imagine the images of that earlier time playing through his mind. "Hey, there used to be a tree over there," he said abruptly. He stared at a neighbor's house across the street, where no tree now stood. "It was a pretty big tree," he said slowly. And then, with a quizzical look on his face, he turned to me. "It was an *apple* tree," he said.

We locked eyes. Oh.

Whether that *particular* apple tree was the subliminal origin of the brand, I cannot say (in the heat of the moment I didn't ask Jobs). But I can state unequivocally that from Steve's parents' humble garage, across the street from that *apple* tree, sprang not only a company destined for greatness, but an entrepreneur destined for greatness as well.

By 1985 Apple had become a Fortune 500 company, thanks to the Apple II and the Mac desktops (which featured a novel controller called a "mouse"). But in 1985 Jobs endured the ultimate humiliation as well: He was forced out of his own company. That alone would be enough for most of us to give up. Yes, he could have hidden himself away in his 14-bedroom mansion. But he didn't. He started NeXT, which pushed Steve's vision of the future of computing so far ahead of then-current markets and expectations that it wasn't until the launch of the Mac OS X (which incorporated NeXT software) that the world could really appreciate how great it was. (Tim Berners-Lee used a NeXT computer to create the first Web server.)

The arc of Jobs's career has been extraordinary ever since, of course: returning in triumph to Apple; buying Pixar and seeing it evolve into a magnet for Academy Awards; the recent success of Apple (despite Jobs's struggle with his health) that led to the iMac, the iPod, the iPhone, and the iPad. Today you can hardly walk into one of the glass-and-chrome Apple stores without feeling the presence of Steve Jobs, as though he might come striding through the door at any moment, his prickly chin turning briskly, his beady eyes scanning the place for things to take apart and make better than they were before.

Vision—that laser beam of foresight that pierces all obstacles: Pasteur, arguing for the existence of microbes. Churchill, calling for fortitude in the face of apparently insurmountable odds. In terms of entrepreneurship, we have the Carnegies, the Edisons, the Fords, all the way up to such present-day icons as Amazon's Jeff Bezos and Google's Larry Page. Visionaries are not only just the stuff of legend. When we string them sequentially, one visionary following another, we have described the arc of history.

What is it that these visionaries have? In fact, what is vision itself? Why do a few of us seem to have this gift? Can we learn it ourselves?

I can give you a few short answers. Visionaries find something that the rest of us have been missing. Jeff Bezos saw his future (and that of Amazon) when he got on a Web site for the first time and learned that the Web population was growing at some 2,000 percent a year. Fred Smith saw it in overnight mail, and soon had Federal Express planes converging on Memphis in the middle of the night. Steve Jobs, of course, recognized the future of personal computing the minute he walked into the Xerox Palo Alto Research Center (PARC) in 1979 and saw the mouse and the graphical user interface.

Visionaries also share a willingness to suffer and struggle for their dreams: Henry Ford, battling a group of powerful businessmen who claimed that they owned a "patent" to the automobile engine (Ford won after taking his fight to the Michigan state supreme court); Edwin Land, the college dropout, lifting an unsecured window at Columbia University at night so that he could slip into the labs to create his first polarization products, the precursors of the Polaroid camera; Hewlett and Packard, working in a garage night after night to build audio-oscillators, voltmeters, and other instruments that paved the way for the electronic age.

When you read the biographies and autobiographies of visionaries, you realize how brutally hard they work, year after year. In the pursuit of their dreams they neglect their health, lose their money, anger their friends and colleagues, and irritate if not alienate their spouses and families. If you're a visionary, history tells us, you probably weren't voted the most popular kid in your class, and, even if you were, you certainly weren't voted the most likely to succeed.

Visionaries are usually depicted looking sternly out over the horizon. One of my favorite such images is the gilded frieze that dominates the entrance to New York City's 30 Rockefeller Plaza (the building that faces the famous ice skating rink and, in December, the iconic Christmas tree). It's a Zeus-like figure that we see there (entitled *Wisdom*). One hand brushes back the clouds of ignorance; the other clutches a golden compass that measures the forces of the cosmos below. Beneath a furrowed brow, his eyes peer forward, and his beard blows against the wind. That's the way we like to think of our visionaries—bigger than life, endowed with superhuman powers. Explorers, pioneers, inventors—they all get the same heroic treatment.

But let me give you a humbler but far more realistic example of the visionary: Dave Thomas, the aw-shucks entrepreneur who gave us, among other things, Wendy's famous hamburgers. In the late 1950s, Thomas was head cook at the Hobby House restaurant in Ft. Wayne, Indiana. One day he was gazing out the window when a big-finned Cadillac pulled up. An elderly man climbed out. He walked spryly around the tail fins, lifted the trunk lid, and began to rummage around. Thomas returned to his cooking. The next thing he knew, the man was standing in front of him. He was a strange sight, sporting a white cotton suit and a black string tie. He had a flowing mustache, a pointed goatee, and patrician-looking white hair that curled up against the back of his collar.[2]

"He introduced himself as a Colonel Harland Sanders," Thomas explained to me one day, "and said he had a secret recipe for cooking chicken. He just happened to have brought a chicken with him and asked if he could use the kitchen." Thomas said yes.

When the Colonel reappeared with his "Kentucky Fried Chicken," Thomas determined that yes, indeed, it was finger-lickin' good. Before long, Dave's boss at the restaurant purchased four of the Colonel's failing franchise restaurants in Columbus, Ohio. Dave was sent to turn them around. He did—cutting the menu from a hundred items to a handful, and introducing the iconic red-and-white KFC chicken bucket (he found some leftover popcorn tubs in the closet and put them to good use). Thus the Kentucky Fried Chicken franchise took wing, and Thomas made his first million. Wendy's was just a few years ahead.

Now, you might say that Dave Thomas was just lucky. But Dave saw something in Colonel Sanders's dream that he liked, and more than that, Dave placed a prescient bet on it.

If you ask visionaries how they do it, they don't provide very satisfactory answers. In fact, most visionaries don't seem to have a clue. "Some of the best ideas just come out of the blue," Virgin Group's Richard Branson has said. "You just have to keep an open mind to see their virtue."[3]

Is it magic, then? I don't think so. Rather, I think the elements of vision are explainable. As I said in the introduction, there are new tools that are helping us understand human behavior better than ever before: Through brain science and cognitive psychology, we have shaped a new lens. By studying visionaries through this lens, we can see, for the first time, how *vision* took Steve Jobs from his garage in Los Altos to the iPhone and iPad, for instance, or how Richard Branson moved from Virgin Records to the Boeing 747s of Virgin Atlantic airlines. How? Well, to explain it, I need to tell you something about the evolution of brain science over the last 30 or 40 years. And to do that, we'll need to see how medicine itself has evolved, and has brought us to the discoveries that we are benefiting from today. Let's start the story at the very beginning, some 2,000 years ago.

From the time of the ancient Greeks, physicians thought the body was made up of a combination of four substances known as humors: yellow bile, black bile, blood, and phlegm. Achieving good health was a matter of adjusting these humors. So if your black bile was too moist, for instance, you'd simply take a laxative of aloe and hellebore—and call your alchemist in the morning.

In 150 A.D. the physician Galen offered some new theories: He noted, for instance, that the heart *cooked* the blood, turning it red; that the blood that rose from the heart to the head was transformed into "animal spirits"; even that the stomach attracted food down the esophagus and turned it into something called chyle. Galen was deemed so astute that for more than a thousand years physicians did little more than quote from Galen's text.[4]

But then Galen's theories began to crumble. In 1537, an anatomist named Andreas Vesalius realized that, for all his fame, Galen had never actually dissected a single *human* corpse. To be sure, he'd split open dogs, pigs, and an occasional goat, but never a person. Vesalius, thanks to a stream of cadavers happily delivered from the gallows by local judges, began to depict the human body as it actually is (Galen had pictured the human womb as similar to that of a dog's, the kidneys like a pig's, and so forth). Vesalius's discoveries were carved into woodblocks for easy replication and distributed throughout the land.

Next, in the 1600s, came the renowned physician William Harvey. Harvey drew a remarkable conclusion for his day: that the heart sends the blood around the body in a loop. "Today we can see that Harvey was to medicine what Galileo was to physics," notes Carl Zimmer in *Soul Made Flesh.* "He reached down into the very core of Galen's account of how the body worked, and showed that it was flawed."

Now mankind was finally on the right track. Subsequent physicians, surgeons, and anatomists were able to detail the human body so precisely that, as the cognitive scientist Steven Pinker notes in *How the Mind Works,* "We understand the body today as a wonderfully complex machine, an assembly of struts, ties, springs, pulleys, levers, joints, hinges, sockets, tanks, pipes, sheaths, pumps, exchangers and filters."[5]

(Physicians continued with their wacky cures, of course. In his autobiography, the writer W. Somerset Maugham recalled as a child [in the 1870s] donkeys arriving at the doorstep of his home every morning: His mother was dying of tuberculosis and the doctors had prescribed fresh donkey's milk. As recently as 1910, the *Merck Manual* advised pure Egyptian mummy for injuries, ground and moistened for application to the wound. Today, we can presume that not a few cures—many of them "new! improved!"—will be reflected upon by future generations with similar disbelief.)

The part of the body that remained a mystery, however, was the brain. While every bodily part seemed to have a mechanical metaphor—be it a spring or lever—what could you say about the brain? It was to all appearances inert: a bowl of curds; a head of cauliflower; a brain coral sleeping silently under the sea.

Galen believed that the brain was a pump that pulsated and drove animal spirits down into the hollow nerves, where they were driven out to the extremities of the body. Harvey, for all his wisdom about the heart, believed that the brain acted as a kind of refrigerator that cooled the blood "lest it be overheated and quickly evanesce . . ." Other physicians and scientists were no closer to the truth. Even as late as the 1950s and 1960s, our understanding of the human brain was far, far behind our understanding of the rest of the human body. And so, the brain remained a mystery.

But then, just about 20 years ago, our knowledge jumped forward. Some of the breakthrough can be traced to the invention of such tools as fMRIs, which can peer inside the brain (and which I will describe later). Much of the new knowledge is also attributable to recent discoveries about neurons and how they function in the brain.

What's remarkable about this breakthrough is that it has attracted not just brain scientists and biologists, but physicists, mathematicians, philosophers, psychiatrists, computer researchers, economists, and engineers as well. The disciplines drawn into this new field of exploration are as diverse as the workings of the human mind itself and form a collaboration of a kind that has never been seen before.

"The day of the mind has come," says University of California philosophy professor Patricia Churchland. "Neuroscience has now developed to a point where many of the traditional questions, which couldn't really be answered by the sciences, are questions which have now moved into the ambit of psychology and neuroscience . . . "[6]

As a result, a not-so-quiet scientific revolution is under way. If you go to any university library, you'll be stunned at the rows and rows of books about neuroscience, cognitive psychology, and neurobiology that sit on the shelves. Periodicals about brain science are legion as well, with scores of titles publishing the latest research in brain science and cognitive science.[7]

Scientific discoveries usually make their first appearance in dry academic papers, then percolate up to textbooks. Few make it all the way to the best-seller list. Not brain science. Go onto Amazon .com, or into a Barnes and Noble or your neighborhood bookstore, and you'll find the shelves piled with books on the subject—often well-written and provocative titles ranging from *Your Brain on Music* and *The Tipping Point* and, yes, *Predictably Irrational*, to such sturdy classics as *Emotional Intelligence, Consciousness Explained, In Search of Memory,* and *The Man Who Mistook His Wife for a Hat.*

In addition to its presence in serious works, brain science has moved into the pop domain. Neuroscientists who a generation ago were sequestered in dusty labs, surrounded by brains floating in bottles, now have celebrity agents, ghostwriters, and regularly scheduled stops on the couches of national talk shows. Popular magazines have turned common emotions (say, falling in love) into explanations of the functions of the brain.

Men's Health magazine recently told readers that the "hormone of horniness" resides in "the hypothalamus, deep in our ancient reptilian brain, and the nearby amygdala, a key to the processing and memory of strong emotions." It added, "Two other hormones flood the brain during intimacy: oxytocin, dubbed the 'cuddle compound,' and vasopressin, a tension-taming peptide that thus far has no catchy nickname."[8]

Now there is a serotonin "power diet" (named for the brain chemical that defuses depression); a rock band named Dopamine (for the brain chemical that fires up ambition); and a brain fitness program called HAPPYneuron (we have some 100 billion neurons in our brains, and some are apparently unhappy).

What is driving this furor of commerce and contemplation? It's not only the discoveries we are making about the brain's biology, but the growing recognition that that biology is the driver of everything we feel, think, and do. The biology of the brain even challenges the question of *who* we are—questions that philosophers have tried to answer over the ages. Let me explain this further.

The connection between the biology of the brain and human behavior was discovered in 1861, with experiments by Paul Broca, a brilliant French surgeon. At the time Broca had a patient who spoke but a few words throughout his life. In the man's last years, Broca studied his speech deficit carefully, and when the patient died, removed his skull. Parting the brain tissue with his forceps, Broca could clearly see the parts of the brain that were injured (in the left frontal lobe), and hence conjectured that those regions (since called Broca's area) were essential to speech.

Next came a German physician, Carl Wernicke. His dying patient could speak but could not *comprehend* speech. During the subsequent autopsy, Wernicke identified the area of injury that caused his patient's deficit: It was the *arcuate fasciculus* (Latin for "curved bundle"), a white fiber that connects the "Broca's area" with an area in the left temporal lobe of the brain (which is now called "Wernicke's area"). Together, these two give humans the ability to speak *and* comprehend. Moreover, the discovery made scientists realize that specific parts of the brain are responsible for very specific functions.[9]

In the ensuing years, scientists learned more from human patients, who were suffering from brain injuries, strokes, epilepsy, Parkinson's, and other afflictions. Antonio Damasio, the David Dornsife Professor of Neuroscience at the University of Southern California, writes that placing an electrode at one point in a patient's brain and delivering a mild current relieved her of the symptoms of Parkinson's disease; placing it two millimeters below that point made her cry, saying that life was hopeless now. The current was shut off—and the patient returned quickly to normal.

In another procedure on a different patient, surgeons were stimulating a region of the left frontal lobe when the patient burst into laughter. "The laugher was so genuine," noted Antonio Damasio, "that the observers described it as contagious." Pretty soon the entire operating room was in stitches. The patient thought everything was funny. When she was shown a picture of a horse, she thought the horse was funny too.[10]

These and other procedures were making clear what scientists already suspected—that there was a relationship not only between the brain and the everyday function of our bodies, but between the brain and our *emotions* as well.

In the 1940s scientists recognized that an atom, placed within a magnetic ring, will vibrate in a unique way that reveals its identity. For that reason, chemists used the process to analyze chemicals. No one had thought of using this property to study the structure of human tissue,[11] but in the early 1970s, Paul Lauterbur, a physical chemist at the State University of New York at Stony Brook, invented what would become the revolutionary tool of neuroscience—the magnetic resonance imaging (MRI) machine. When Lauterbur submitted his idea in an article to the scientific journal *Nature,* it was rejected. But that didn't stop him (he later told the *New York Times,* "You could write the entire history of science in the last few years in terms of papers rejected by *Science* or *Nature*"). In the end, his work was not only accepted, but he won the Nobel Prize for it in 2003.[12]

Today the MRI machine is a familiar piece of hospital equipment. Color images of the brain's structure, similar in appearance to the Doppler radar maps we see in weather reports, have changed the way we diagnose neurological disorders. Functional MRI (fMRI), a newer development, allows live "movies" of the brain in action. The movies show blood rushing to the various parts of the brain, refreshing the neurons with new supplies of oxygen.[13]

Mapping the brain is one thing. But how do all these regions of the brain come together to make *us*? As I noted earlier, metaphors were found for the rest of the body: The heart is a pump. The kidneys, a filter. The lungs, a bellows. The eyes are lenses with adjustable apertures. But what metaphor could possibly describe the workings of the brain?

Nothing would do, until just recently. And then it appeared—the most remarkable metaphor of them all: the computer.

This part of our story begins with Alan Turing, who in 1934 had just graduated in mathematics from King's College at Cambridge University. Just two years later he published a remarkable paper, "On Computable Numbers," which effectively anticipated the modern-day computer. Turing had contemplated the way in which a mathematician solved a problem. As he reviewed the numbers of ways that humans come to any conclusion, he realized that step-by-step logic could be represented by a sequence of elementary computations.[14] He started with *IF* and *THEN*: "*If* I get good grades on my papers, *Then* I will receive an A in class." Or: "*If* I get good grades on my papers, *And* my attendance is unbroken, *Then* I will get an A in the class." Turing then transferred this insight into a hypothetical device that could scan a paper tape to see if a 0 or a 1 was written on it. Reflecting the steps of human logic, it could erase the 0 (or 1), or change it, or leave it as it was. His idea led to the creation of the on/off binary code that serves as the language of software and computers.[15]

In the 1940s, John von Neumann, considered one of the twentieth century's most brilliant mathematicians, took Turing's idea and reworked it as a *real machine*—with the data storage and interchangeable software that we recognize in computers today. That's not all. Von Neumann also recognized that the 0s and 1s of computers are similar to the functioning of the brain itself. "It is worth noticing," he wrote in the summer of 1945, "that the neurons of the higher animals . . . have all-or-none character, that is, two states: quiescent and excited." He added, "It is easily seen that these simplified neuron functions can be imitated by telegraphic relays or by vacuum tubes."[16]

In other words, the brain and the computer appeared to process information in pretty much the same way. This is what became known as the computational theory of the mind. With it, researchers began to look at the brain in a new way. In particular, they began to focus on the brain's neurons. "Neurons are the cells essential for brain activity," explains USC's Antonio Damasio. The fascinating thing about neurons is that they actually switch off and on, similar to the binary code of computers and Turing's 0s and 1s: When a neuron receives an excitatory signal, it fires a minute electric charge; when it receives an inhibitory signal, it becomes less likely to fire. When clumps of neurons fire (or don't), their combined actions create a physical reaction (such as the movement of a finger) or even an emotional one. Very simply, then, the theory posits that the great complexity of human thought and action begins as simply as 0s and 1s.

You might wonder how the complexity of the human mind, with its palette of emotions and intellect, could arise from such a simple arrangement. But when you consider that humans have 100 billion neurons, and that each of these neurons has between 1 and 10,000 synapses (synapses are the connecting points from which the electric charges from the neurons go out across the brain), the computing potential of the brain becomes remarkably large. In fact, if one considers all the possible ways that our 100 billion neurons could be wired, the sum comes to 10 followed by at least a million zeros. That's quite a few connections, considering that the number of particles in the known universe is 10 followed by 79 zeros.[17]

In *The Quest for Consciousness,* California Institute of Technology professor Christof Koch notes, "Conscious perception is based on synchronous-firing neuronal assemblies that wax and wane rhythmically and interact with each other within a few hundred milliseconds."[18] In other words, all these neurons work together with a rhythm, and from that comes intelligence and, moreover, consciousness. And from that comes thinking, and human life.

In the following pages, then, let's use the lens of brain science and cognitive psychology to take a look at the most remarkable of all kinds of human beings—the visionary. We see them in our midst—we make icons of them and put them on magazine covers. They seem to see what the rest of us don't see. They seem to predict the future. And they seem almost infallible, with success after success. Along the way, we'll learn something new about them—and, just as important, something about ourselves.

2

CHAPTER TWO

Awakening

My first encounter with Richard Branson came at his home office. But in no way did it resemble either a home or an office: It was a creaky old houseboat, in a line of houseboats tied up along a canal towpath in the London suburb of Maida Vale.

To get to the *Duende* (for that's what she was called), you had to duck under several branches and the occasional clothesline strung between the trees bordering the towpath. She was humble, with two bedrooms and a living area that Branson had fitted with two comfortable chairs and a rug.

I called out from down below, heard a shout from above, and climbed the ladder. As my head cleared the upper deck I had my first view of the man: He was stripped to the waist on this pleasant summer day, his feet propped up on a round patio table upon which two telephones sat. One foot was bare and the other sheathed in a tattered athletic sock, from which his big toe boldly protruded.[1]

Branson shot me his now-famous smile and beckoned to me to have a seat. He was chatting animatedly over the phone with his father, a country barrister whom Branson clearly adored. Branson had lived on the canal for years. It was from this unlikely location that he had orchestrated the success of his Virgin mail-order record business (his second enterprise, following the failure of his student newspaper), and from here as well that he and his cousin Simon Draper had started Virgin Records and made their first fortune with Virgin's first album, *Tubular Bells.*

It was aboard the *Duende* as well that Branson held his meetings— with both bankers and bands like the Sex Pistols. It was here that he courted and won his wife Joan, and it was to the *Duende* one November morning in 1981 that he and Joan brought home their newborn daughter Holly.

We hit it off that afternoon, drinking wine and watching the narrow canal boats glide past us on the sparkling water. A few days later he called me, wondering if I'd like to go out to The Manor. Every tycoon needs a manor, and Branson had found his early on. It was in 1971; he was thumbing through *Country Life* magazine when his gaze fell upon a sixteenth-century home at Shipton-on-Cherwell, about an hour's drive north of London. Offered for 35,000 pounds, Branson got it for 30,000 (his aunt pitched in with a 10,000-pound loan).[2]

Branson soon turned The Manor into a comfortable recording studio. Paul and Linda McCartney dropped in to record *Band on the Run;* the Stones frolicked with their girlfriends and laid down tracks there; Boy George recorded his hit records at The Manor as well.

Branson picked me up in London and we headed for The Manor. Arriving in the long summer dusk, I saw an outline of turrets and lights glowing softly from behind diamond-paned windows. We didn't drive up the gravel driveway; instead, on Branson's whim, we left the car near the road and sprinted over a wooden fence and across a meadow to the house. As we approached the front door, Branson pointed to the stone lintel and warned me to watch my head—The Manor was built in the time of Charles I, when people were shorter, he said. Inside, the hallway and rooms were furnished with antiques and velvet drapes.

Earlier, I had gleaned an important insight into the mind of a visionary. As we were driving up to The Manor I mentioned that once, while I was at the *Wall Street Journal,* I had interviewed a CEO whose company had just invested a great amount of money in a New York skyscraper. I'd asked the man how many stories the building had. The CEO hadn't a clue. I said to Branson, Isn't that silly? You've bought a skyscraper and you don't even know how *tall* it is?

Branson hesitated—he didn't want to rebuke me—but then replied somewhat sternly that if you're running a company, it's the *vision* that counts, not the details. In fact, he continued, you *cannot* grow a company if you are bogged down in the nuts and bolts. I remember feeling abashed at having brought it up. That was a significant lesson, I realized, but the lesson wasn't over yet.

A few weeks later Branson invited me up to his weekend retreat, Mill End, in Oxfordshire, England, a lovely Tudor home with a softly thatched roof. Out front, wild waterfowl paddled and splashed among the tall reeds of a marshy moat.

Inside, I met a few other guests. We sat in the expansive living room for a while and then were ushered into a courtyard, where we had a lovely lunch, another great conversation, and—as always around Branson—a lot of horseplay and laughs. Following lunch we went back to the living room. At this point, one of the guests, a curly-haired Frenchman named Julien Clerc, handed a tape to Branson, who proceeded to put it into his tape player. Clerc, unbeknownst to me, was one of the biggest singers in France, something like a Neil Diamond or even a Paul McCartney. Later, when I mentioned to a French woman that I had dined with Clerc, she was astounded. Julien Clerc! But since I was oblivious to his fame at the time, I conversed with Clerc with what he must have considered refreshing nonchalance.

As the tape began to play—it was Clerc's new song, we were told—everyone in the high-ceilinged living room responded appreciatively. It was a lively number, and as I looked around the room, I saw everyone tapping their feet and swaying with the song. With one exception: Branson. He still had a smile on his face, but I noticed that he wasn't tapping his foot. In fact, he had an increasingly glazed look in his eye.[3]

As I looked at him, I thought about our earlier conversation, about how one mustn't focus on the details. So here it was: Branson, the music mogul, not even tapping his toe! But having said that, and with the benefit of hindsight, I think something else was going on—something that has a lot to do with how visionaries find their way to their big ideas. If you're looking for what makes a visionary tick, what follows offers an important clue.

As I noted earlier, the human brain is extraordinarily good at spotting patterns. It has to be: It's accosted with something like 11 million pieces of information a second (based on the number of receptor cells of each sense organ and the nerves that go from these cells to our brains). That's information from the eyes, the ears, the nose, even the skin. Every part of the body is continuously absorbing information and sending it to the brain.

But we also create our own confusion. Take speech. Suppose you wanted to create a twenty-word sentence, and had ten possibilities for each of the twenty words (ten choices for the first word, ten for the second word, and so on). How many different sentences could you create? Two thousand? Ten thousand? The answer is ten to the twentieth power, or a hundred million trillion (or 100 times the number of seconds since the birth of the universe). The choices for expressing yourself, if you had to start from scratch every time you opened your mouth, are nearly endless.[4]

Now here's the rub: In 1956 psychologist George A. Miller determined that most people can hold only seven pieces of information in their short-term memory at a time. (It's a simple test: Give someone a set of numbers to repeat. Most people will remember between seven and nine of them.) But if we have billions of pieces of data flying at us, and we can remember only seven to nine discrete things, how in the world do we get along? The answer is that the brain takes endless bits of data and deftly puts them into patterns.[5]

For example, suppose I asked you to remember and repeat this string of letters: WSRFNEUOL. That would be difficult. Then suppose I asked you to remember the same letters in this order: SUNFLOWER. It makes all the difference in the world. And that's why telephone numbers are not 8435551075, but 843-555-1075. By breaking up the digits, we give the brain a better chance to remember the entire sequence. We also use mnemonic aids in many applications—such as the phrase Good Boys Do Fine Always for remembering the bass clef musical note sequence GBDFA. And in speech we are hardwired with syntax, which creates rules for converting thought into speech.

It is the pattern, then, that lets us remember things. How did Ron King of Barbados set a record in the game of checkers in 1998 by beating 385 players in just 3 hours and 44 minutes? He had memorized so many checkers patterns that he needed but a glance at the boards to win the game.[6] Chess players rely on patterns as well. Good players have 1,000 patterns in their memory; masters are said to have 50,000 and more. We all seek patterns, and when we can't find them—when we "just don't get it"—we feel uncomfortable. We experience physical pain. But when we figure the problem out, there is relief; the brain may even give us a celebratory squirt of dopamine.[7]

But it's not the *number* of patterns that account for visionary insight; it's the *quality* of the patterns. The patterns that a visionary is seeking are not that easy to unscramble. Productive thinking is like cognitive rock climbing. Once visionaries get to the first pattern, they force themselves to climb higher up the rock face— to see the second pattern, and then the third. At each stage they climb higher, and set their gaze farther.

I found the clearest explanation of this, oddly, in the autobiography of one of Madison Avenue's advertising "Mad Men." Moreover, this Mad Man was a woman. Her name was Shirley Polykoff, and in the three-martini-lunch era of such advertising giants as David Ogilvy and Bill Bernbach, Polykoff held her own as arguably the smartest copywriter in New York City. Polykoff's biggest success was with Miss Clairol, the hair-lightening product. How did she do it? Polykoff had a knack for finding the highest, most sublime thought—pushing from one pattern up to the next—until she found the emotional hook that made the idea sing. What is Clairol? Hair dye. What's the higher thought than that? It lightens your hair. What's the higher thought than that? *Blondes have more fun.*[8]

That line sent thousands of women running to the store (and even caused a sensation in the gloomy USSR, where the Clairol "Is it true blondes have more fun?" jingle became an underground hit). But it's also a concise reminder of the sequential thinking that builds an idea higher and higher. That's why you'll often find visionaries staring—blankly—out the window. Or at the wall. Or, as Branson was fond of doing, pacing slowly around the pond at Mills End, staring vacantly at the birds and reeds. They're trying to raise the pattern to the next level.

But what pattern *exactly* is the visionary looking for? Here is where it gets really interesting. To convey this properly, however, let me take you inside one of the most exclusive clubs for visionaries in the world.

The Institute for Advanced Study in Princeton, New Jersey, is probably America's most famous think tank. A stark concrete and glass building outside, with birch trees in the courtyard, its interior has a Scandinavian feel, with slate floors and maple trim. The math genius Alan Turing spent a number of years here in the 1930s. Einstein did, too, serving as a faculty member from 1933 until his death in 1955. There are a couple of bronze sculptures in his honor in the public areas. It was said that Einstein would bring his violin to his little office at the Institute, and that you could hear him scratching out a tune from time to time. An amusing thought: Einstein tearing up the catgut while everyone else is trying to think. Albert!

At the Institute, the food is superb. A French-trained sous-chef prepares meals under the eye of an executive chef. Every afternoon at four, little cakes and coffee are served in the lounge. At that hour most of the deep thinkers come out of their quite homey (but small) offices to mingle. It's a very comfortable existence. Most of the intellectuals stay as long as they can. A few have never left.

I spent several days at the Institute recently with MIT (now Duke) professor Dan Ariely. We were writing a book together called *Predictably Irrational*. One day Dan, who is always brimming with tricks, asked me if I'd like to participate in a little experiment. After I was assured I wouldn't be wired up to a machine like a laboratory rat, I cautiously agreed.

Dan sat me in front of his computer. He said I was going to see a short film clip of people moving around and passing a basketball. I was to count how many times the ball passed from person to person. Since Dan was a brilliant MIT professor and I was not, and since he had been considered a deep enough thinker to receive an invitation to the Institute (and I had not—in fact, I was sleeping in Dan's kid's bedroom, surrounded by stuffed toys), I decided to impress him with my best effort. I stared intently at the screen and counted carefully.

When I told Dan how many times the ball passed from player to player, he laughed heartily.

Didn't you see the gorilla?

What gorilla?

He ran the film clip again. *Now* I saw it. Right in the middle of the game someone in a full-body gorilla suit came dancing through the players—even beating his chest aggressively at center stage. I was counting the ball passes so intently that I had missed the gorilla entirely.

What Dan showed me was a now-famous experiment by Daniel J. Simons and Christopher F. Chabris of Harvard's psychology department. It was designed to show that when we are actively looking for what we expect, we become blind to what is right before our eyes.[9]

There have been several variations on this experiment. In one, the viewer is asked to press a button every time a team of basketball players passes the ball between them. In the midst of this, a woman strolls across the screen holding an open umbrella. Of twenty-eight observers in this particular study, only six reported the presence of the umbrella woman.

Although the gorilla experiment may strike you as silly, it demonstrates something of profound importance: The most remarkable things in this world are here, now, right before us. The problem is that we just don't see them. Or, as Chabris and Simons note in their best seller *The Invisible Gorilla,* "We experience far less of our visual world than we think we do."[10]

Consider this riddle:

> *In a marble hall white as milk*
> *Lined with skin as soft as silk*
> *Within a fountain crystal-clear*
> *A golden apple doth appear.*

No doors there are to this stronghold,
Yet thieves break in to steal its gold.[11]

Have you racked your mind to find the answer? Are these meaningless words, or do they form a thought? The answer is right before you. What can it be? Well, it's nothing more complicated than an egg. Of course! The answer was there all along, right in front of your nose.

How often is the answer right there with you? If you were walking through any European or American city in the eighteenth century, you might have teased out a similar puzzle of far greater portent: people dying of typhoid fever, anthrax, cholera, diphtheria, gonorrhea, tetanus, pneumonia, meningitis, dysentery, plague, botulism, whooping cough.

What is the gorilla dancing through this macabre eighteenth-century scene? Bacteria. It was there, in front of everyone's eyes. But it took visionary microbe hunters like Robert Koch, armed with increasingly more powerful microscopes, to realize it. Once they did, the precise bacteria responsible for each of these diseases were found within two decades.

The same puzzles await solving today. Only the names—multiple sclerosis, cancer, autism, and more—have changed.

This makes an important point about visionaries: They don't need to see what *doesn't* exist to change the world. They just need to see what's *here* but unseen by others.

Once I had to review several years' worth of *BusinessWeek* magazines (while writing a book with one of the former governors of the Federal Reserve). As I leafed through one issue after the next, starting in 1998 and moving forward, I was struck by the number of warnings we should have seen that an economic storm was building: massive inventories, unlimited confidence, even the creation of a new concept—the New Economy—to rationalize what was really irrational behavior. I found that, during this period, *BusinessWeek*'s "Business Outlook" columnists, James C. Cooper and Kathleen Madigan, were incredibly prescient. The gorilla was dancing before their eyes—and they saw it. And yet for most of us, the dot-com bust came down unexpectedly.

We needn't go back a decade for an example, however. In early 2007, while the Dow was still climbing toward its peak of 14,000, the banks were flush, and consumer confidence was sky high, Nassim Nicholas Taleb had just published his brilliant and compelling book *The Black Swan*. In the book, he warned, "Almost all banks are now interrelated. So the financial economy is swelling into gigantic, incestuous, bureaucratic banks—when one falls, they all fall." He also worried about J.P. Morgan's use of risk management, which he called a "phony method of aiming to manage risk," one that "puts the whole world at risk."

And as for government-sponsored Fannie Mae, wrote Taleb, "When I look at their risks, they seem to be sitting on a barrel of dynamite, vulnerable to the slightest hiccup. But not to worry: their large staff of scientists deemed these events 'unlikely.' "

And so what exactly was the gorilla dancing before Taleb's eyes? "We have moved from a diversified ecology of small banks, with varied lending policies," he wrote, "to a more homogenous framework of firms that all resemble one another. True, we now have fewer failures, but when they occur . . . I shiver at the thought."[12] That was in 2006. What bigger gorilla did we need to see?

The point is that visionaries don't see what *doesn't* exist. They see what is *here* but transparent to our eyes. It reminds me of the Buddhist teaching: When asked if he were a god or a man, the Buddha replied, neither. "I am awake," he said. So is a visionary.

And so, as we listened to the Clerc song in Branson's living room, I first thought that Branson's absent stare was proof of what he had told me in the car—that details would sink the visionary.

But now I realize it was more than that: Bronson was puzzling out one of the most visionary moves of his career, one that would transform Virgin.

As he writes in his autobiography, "A number of people started suggesting ideas to us that would have increased Virgin's exposure in entertainment, but my imagination was really captured by a proposal that came entirely out of the blue . . . In February 1984 an American lawyer called Randolph Fields asked me whether I was interested in operating an airline . . ."[13] Branson says that Fields sent him the proposal, which he brought up to Mills End to read.

So as we sat together that evening, Branson had already agreed to go into the airline business. The marketing had begun. But to everyone's surprise, the response from the public was far greater and more encouraging than anyone had imagined. Thousands of travelers were booking reservations. The press was in love with the idea. Columnists were predicting that Branson's airline would break the grip of British Airways and the other traditional carriers on transcontinental flight. It would change the face of air travel in Europe, and possibly America as well.

The stars were settling into a pattern, and Branson was struggling to see how they were about to align. He had to awaken himself—like the Buddha—to seize the day.

At that moment, Shirley Polykoff might have coached him to raise his thinking incrementally to the highest level: Terminals and airplanes make what? Which means *what*? And what does *that* mean?

How do we answer those questions? How do we see the pattern that is dancing before us? Fortunately the brain has given us all a marvelous pattern recognition tool: It's our ability to move images around in our minds—*pictures* of things. We needn't be blind, then, for the brain has given us the ability to *see*.

Seeing

Imagine the Eiffel Tower.

Now zoom in for a close-up. Examine a single girder. See the heads of the rivets, the clean corners of the steel.

Okay, zoom out. Now raise the whole thing in the air. Turn it around slowly, letting the sunshine strike each side. Now put it back into the ground. For a finale, let the night fall like a curtain, throw some stars into the sky, bathe the Eiffel Tower in purple light, and set some fireworks off all around.

Okay, how did we do that?

We have no viewing room in the brain, after all—no auditorium with projector and screen. No paint cans set on a long shelf. No stock photos of the Eiffel Tower/close-ups/late afternoon.

Yet what an expressive instrument our vision is. Not only can we create images, we can scan across them, zoom in and out, paste, join, and superimpose. We can even escape reality: Let's disassemble the Eiffel Tower and reshape its girders from a triangle to a square—or give it legs and have it leap across the English Channel.

"Pyramids, cathedrals, and rockets exist not because of geometry, theory of structures, or thermodynamics, but because they were first pictures—literally visions—in the minds of those who conceived them," wrote history professor Eugene Ferguson in *Engineering and the Mind's Eye*. "Usually the significant governing decisions regarding an artisan's or an engineer's design have been made before the artisan picks up [his] tools or the engineer turns to his drawing board."[1] He adds, "The mind's eye is the organ in which a lifetime of sensory information—visual, tactile, muscular, visceral, aural, olfactory, and gustatory—is stored, interconnected, and interrelated."

To be sure, what we're seeing isn't a real picture. It's a mental representation, drawn from the memory. Some neuroscientists believe that specific neurons respond to particular objects or concepts. Others say that an image is distributed throughout the brain.

In a particularly interesting experiment, neurosurgeon Itzhak Fried at the University of California at Los Angeles implanted an electrode into a single neuron in a patient's amygdala (the amygdala receives input from the visual cortical areas). What was remarkable was that this single neuron fired an electric charge every time it detected a picture of President Bill Clinton—regardless of whether the patient was viewing an official portrait of Clinton, a snapshot of Clinton on a receiving line, or even a pencil sketch. That particular neuron didn't respond to anything else presented to the patient—not a picture of Michael Jordan, or of a scorpion, a colonial plantation house, a New York Street scene, or photographs of several other presidents. What this suggests (in addition to the fact that the neuron is obviously a Democrat) is that at least part of a memory can be impressed upon a single neuron.[2]

Not everyone agrees with the single-neuron theory, even if it encompasses a cluster of neurons in tight proximity. Neuroscientist Antonio Damasio argues, for instance, that "Aunt Maggie as a complete person does not exist in one single site of your brain. She's distributed all over it."³

Wherever Aunt Maggie is located—or scattered, for that matter— the important point is that from fMRI studies, scientists now see that *imaginary* images (say, our memory of Aunt Maggie in her floral dress) are processed in the same part of the brain that processes the visual image. When we *look* at something, in other words, the *same* part of the brain lights up as when we *imagine* that something. This is called the "mutual interference" between imagery and perception.

If you want to prove this to yourself, take a look at your cell phone. Now, while staring at it, try to *imagine* your phone. You probably can't do it. Why? Because the part of your brain that is *looking* at your phone (the visual cortex) is the same part required to *imagine* your phone. Now look at your phone and then lift your eyes off into the distance. There it is—in your mind's eye. Why? Because your brain, freed of the visual image, is able to re-create the imagined image in your brain.⁴

This demonstrates how true our imagination is to the outside world: Pianists who *imagine* playing a piece on the piano activate the same part of their brains (the frontal parietal network) as when they actually press the keys.⁵ Similarly, when vision is destroyed in one area, it is destroyed in the other. A stroke patient who has lost the ability to see color, for instance, also can't imagine in color.⁶ In *The Man Who Mistook His Wife for a Hat,* neurologist Oliver Sacks describes a man who could see perfectly well, but whose cortex was damaged. Not only could he not *imagine* things any longer, he could no longer *dream* with imagery either—the message of the dream being conveyed in nonvisual terms, such as words and sounds.⁷

But it's not just objects that flicker about in our minds; ideas do as well. Most of the words we use in our "inner" speech—before speaking or writing a sentence—exist as auditory or visual images in our consciousness.[8] Nouns, it seems, are stored as visual memories, and verbs as spatial relations among the words. Ideas in this form can be moved around and examined from different aspects.[9] Since visions and ideas are constantly fading out—continuously clearing out of the memory buffer—anything that one wants to chew over to any extent must be consciously, and with some effort, tossed back into the mind.

In *Consciousness Explained,* philosopher Dan Dennett describes thinking as a continuous process of mulling and recapitulation. "Contents arise, get revised, contribute to the interpretation of other contents or to the modulation of behavior," he writes, "and in the process leave their traces in the memory, which then eventually decay or get incorporated or overwritten by later contents, wholly or in part."[10]

And so we carry these images and ideas in our heads, and most of us are incessantly tinkering with them. The visionaries, of course, work their imaginations on the things that matter to them the most. "I carry my thoughts about me for a long time, often a very long time, before writing them down," Beethoven told a friend. "I change many things, discard others, and try again and again until I am satisfied; then, in my head, I begin to elaborate the work in its breadth, its narrowness, its height, its depth . . . I hear and see the image in front of me from every angle, as if it had been cast (like a sculpture), and only the labor of writing it down remains."[11]

Elmer Sperry, the creator of the Sperry gyroscope and more than 400 other patented inventions, from an electric car to high-intensity searchlights, was said to stare at phantoms that seemed just a few feet from his eyes. A veteran of the Sperry Gyroscope Company recalled the way that Sperry would be "just looking into the air, when all at once he would pick up a pad and hold it at arm's length, then with a pencil in the other hand he would begin to draw." It would take several iterations to get the product right on paper—but the seminal idea was there all along, floating before his eyes.[12]

Walt Disney saw images in his head, but he also visualized the steps required to move his business ahead. "No matter how good a picture we turn out, I can always see ways to improve it when I see the final product," he wrote in his 1934 autobiography.[13] For visionaries, *seeing* is everything.

I was six stories belowground, at the particle accelerator site of CERN, the European Organization for Nuclear Research and its laboratory for particle physics in Geneva, Switzerland. In the huge subterranean chamber sat one of the biggest science experiments of all time, a 2,000-ton machine as large as a house, with hundreds of thick electric cables running to it. I was at one of three viewing stations for what at the time was the world's largest particle accelerator, a device four miles in circumference. It is capable of hurling two beams of particles—one of protons, one of antiprotons— against each other at nearly the speed of light.[14]

Shortly before I arrived in 1984, a group of CERN scientists had discovered two elemental particles never seen before—field particles W and Z, as they were dubbed. Now, like big-game hunters, the scientists were firing up the atom smasher again, this time in the hunt for an even more elusive type of quarry: strange, fundamental forces of matter called quarks.

I didn't expect CERN to be as big as it is. But in fact it is a sprawling complex, straddling the French-Swiss border and employing thousands of scientists, engineers, and technicians. With its cavernous underground rooms filled with scientific equipment and its hordes of busy workers, CERN resembles the kind of secret laboratory that James Bond is always blowing up at the end of his films.

As my days passed in the underground rooms, I met a number

of the physicists involved in the project. They all spoke passionately of the quest, their English laced with the accents of their homelands—France, Germany, Italy, Spain. I dutifully wrote down what they said, but as I reviewed my notes, I found little that made a good story. I was looking for a "hook," that bit of magic that makes a newspaper story—and particularly a front-page *Wall Street Journal* story—sing.

My time at CERN was running short when I noticed a different breed of man. He strode the halls beneath the ground with the swagger of a Roman general—in fact, his long coat hung majestically from his shoulders like a cape. He was impressively tall and big-boned, with a loose piece of forelock that swung over his face. Following him, I slipped into one of the underground meeting rooms.

There he was, at the lectern, with the other scientists sitting before him like schoolchildren in class. He asked one of them to rise and deliver a report. As the young scientist rose and nervously began his presentation, the Roman general grew sullen. He turned his back to the group and scrawled some equations on the board. When the young scientist had finished, the general whipped his head around. He was angry. His voice boomed. He turned to the equations on the board and slapped at them angrily with his wooden ruler. His eyes swept the faces in the audience. "This is crap," he declared.

At that moment I realized that whoever this fellow was, I had found my story for the *Journal*. That impression was amplified after the meeting, when I had the opportunity to talk with him. The other scientists had spoken passionately about the project, but used detail that I frankly couldn't follow. This man, however, spoke *vividly* as well. "When W and Z particles crash together," he said, with an explosive clap of his hands, "things never seen on earth before—purple giraffes and two-headed zebras—spring from the fire."

His eyes flew open, his face flushed with emotion. His glasses reflected the image of the machinery behind us. For the first time I saw what the experiment was about—what would happen when the particles slammed into each other at the speed of light, liberating matter that would exist for a billionth of a trillionth of a second before exploding into subatomic fragments.

As it turned out, I had stumbled upon the Italian physicist Carlo Rubbia. Rubbia's particular genius lies not only in his gift for metaphor and simile, but also in his powers of visualization. "When you dive into matter, it's as exciting as making an infinitely long interplanetary journey," he told an interviewer several years later. "You can *see* things happening not on a large scale, but on smaller and smaller scales. You get more and more details, and new pictures come in your mind one after another."[15]

Rubbia worked his team relentlessly. He drove them to create a machine that no one thought could be built, a machine that found the W and Z subatomic particles. In 1984, shortly after my visit, and in recognition of those achievements, he won the Nobel Prize in physics.

Rubbia wasn't the only Nobel Prize winner who had pictures in his mind as he pursued his visionary quest. Shortly after meeting Rubbia, I went to a London pub, where, waiting for me, was Sir James Black. Sir James had invented several of the world's best-selling drugs, including beta blockers (used to treat angina and high blood pressure) and cimetidine, otherwise known as the stomach-acid killer Tagamet. Knighted in 1981, Sir James won the Nobel in medicine in 1987.

Sir James and I spoke for quite a while about his teen years in London during the Blitz. He recalled the German V-1 rockets crossing the channel and entering the city. "That must have been terrible, when you heard them approaching," I said. "Oh, it wasn't *then* that you had to worry," he replied. "It was when you suddenly heard *nothing*. Then you knew the engine had cut off, and it was plunging down on top of you."

In explaining his success as a researcher, Sir James said visualization played a critical role. He was always imagining chemical compounds, turning the parts of the molecules around in his head, he said. In fact, Sir James once told Lewis Wolpert, professor of biology at University College, London, "I daydream like mad . . . You can have all these structures in your head turning and tumbling and moving."

"So you daydream chemical structures?" Wolpert asked incredulously.

"Oh yes," Sir James replied brightly. "You make a number of assumptions. You assume that the receptor doesn't know any more about chemistry than chemists do, and you then try and pretend that you are a receptor. You imagine what it would be like if this molecule was coming out of space toward you. What would it look like, what would it do?"[16]

It's not unusual: Einstein said that in pursuing his famous theory of relativity, he tried to imagine what it would be like to ride on a beam of light. Richard Feynman, the physicist, made his discoveries in quantum physics by asking, "If I were an electron, what would I do?"[17]

Is visualization the province of geniuses? Or can we all see to some extent with our mind's eye? That was the question that occurred to Sir Francis Galton one day. Galton was a British intellectual with a broad range of scientific interests: He published the first weather map (in the London *Times* in 1875); he devised a method for classifying fingerprints that gave birth to forensic science; he made comparative measurements of people's faces and coined the term eugenics—and with it, the phrase "nature versus nurture"; he was also the first to explain the technique of regression to the mean, in which a phenomenon that is at the extreme in its first measurement will tend to be closer to the mean in the next measurement.

In 1883 Galton began to ponder how well we visualize things. Do some of us have better visualization skills than others? Do we walk around with a fuzzy, gray picture of imagined things, while others see them in sharp, vivid color?[18]

One day, Galton wrote a letter to his friends, asking them if they would report just how much they remembered from the previous day's breakfast. The request was the first time that anyone had tried to determine the clarity and vividness of imagination with some measure of scientific rigor. "Is the image dim or fairly clear?" he wrote. "Is its brightness comparable to the actual scene?" And what about the definition? "Are all the objects pretty well defined at the same time, or is the place of sharpest definition at any one moment more contracted than it is in the real scene?"

Coloring was important as well. "Are the colours of the china, of the toast, the bread-crust, mustard, meat, parsley, whatever may have been eaten at the table, quite distinct and natural?" he asked.

What he found was a range of vividness. Some people could see the breakfast table in what seemed like remarkable clarity: The blue flowerwork on the teapot; the engravings on the shimmering silver; the rich yellow of the egg yolk; the light washing across the breakfast table; the girl, her hair up in ribbons; and the boy leaning across for the toast. Their recall was like a photograph, as though they were seeing it rather than remembering it.

Others saw just a few items on the breakfast table. Still others saw a gray veil upon it all. A few saw no pictures at all. "Zero," replied one. "I recollect the breakfast table but do not see it."

Galton had stumbled on a remarkable aspect of human consciousness: Some people seem to be natural visionaries. Their imaginations *are* sharper and more vivid than normal. By comparison, the rest of us are remembering our lives with a fuzzy 1950s TV.

As soon as Galton reported his findings, there were questions. Since the participants had to self-assess their own visualization skills (no one could look into their minds), some of them might have been more generous in scoring the quality of their visual insight than others. In other words, some may have had more active imaginations than the rest.

But subsequent studies brought out a finding that was even more surprising, and certainly counterintuitive: People who claimed to be able to construct vivid mental images were not necessarily better at taking those images and actually *doing something* with them. They were not necessarily able, for instance, to move the teapot around in their minds, so that the spout was where the handle was, and vice versa. And when it came to tests that demonstrated a person's ability to detect patterns or find similarities in objects that had been rotated, people who reported seeing *no* vivid images did just as well as everyone else.

Further studies (the "Questionnaire Upon Mental Imagery" developed by Columbia University professor G. H. Betts in 1909, and the "Vividness of Visual Imagery Questionnaire" developed by British psychologist David Marks in 1973) showed that although vivid imaginers generally remember the *colors* of things better than the rest of us, they don't have a superior memory overall. They may recall that the sedan that crashed into the neighbor's yard was green, but they don't remember the other details any better than the rest of us.[19]

So for the visionary, then, what really counts? Apparently it's not a matter of whether your internal imagery is HDTV or static-laden black-and-white. Rather, it is your ability to snap apart the components of an image, rotate them, bend them, fold them, and—most important—scan them from different angles of perspective.

This, beyond the brightness of the image or its clarity, distinguishes the transformational thinking of visionaries. The brain that can construct a visual image, retain it in working memory, transform it, and compare it to other images in the working memory—that's a marvelous thinking machine.

With the tools of spatial vision, then, we can dismantle, reorient, and reassemble the parts of the physical world. Take a look at your phone again. Now look away. Imagine it spinning in the air, the straps floating along. Make its face a rectangle. This falls in the realm of what neuroscientists call the working memory, a tool bench where we can shape everything that's hanging around—new memories, old memories, images fresh from the outside world, even waves of emotion.

Look at your cell phone again. We've already determined that most of us can't imagine a cell phone while we're looking at it. But you can imagine things *around* it. Let's give it a pair of curly little antennas protruding from the sides. See them? Now, can you lift the entire image from your hand and imagine it floating in air, antennas and all?

The particular struggle in all of this is that our consciousness is transitory. After about three seconds it dumps whatever it has and refreshes the mind with new thoughts. Trying to hold on to an image—long enough, at least, to make some sense of it—is difficult. You might have just reset the antennas on your imaginary wristwatch when the darned thing begins to fade away.

It takes skill to imagine something—and then to cling to that imagined object long enough to turn it from thin air into substance. But that is the trick at which visionaries excel. Let me tell you about one of them.

Several years ago I drove up a winding road in Redwood City, California, to a house set precipitously on the side of a hill. Once inside, I waited with the babysitter for a half an hour until Jeff Hawkins, with wife, kids, and dogs, came bursting in the front door.[20] Hawkins, you may know, invented the PalmPilot a few years ago, the first successful handheld computer.

Hawkins grew up on the North Shore of Long Island, New York, near the Jakobson Shipyard, which was one of the big shipbuilding facilities on the East Coast. Something about being that close to the shipyard had infected his family, because in their spare time they all designed and built boats. And not just any kind of boat. Hawkins remembers with fondness one of his favorites: Named the *Sea Space,* it was sixteen-sided and had a fabric skirt. When it reached the edge of a beach, the family would lower its wooden legs to the sand, extend the gangplank, and make themselves at home.[21]

Hawkins grew up with hands roughed up by fiberglass resin and wood. But in high school his interest turned to math and physics. He eventually wound up at Cornell University to study electrical engineering. After a short stop at GRiD Systems, a small computer company, and Intel, he went on to graduate school at the University of California at Berkeley, where he studied neurobiology, wrote a thesis on auto-associative memories (that was rejected), and found himself out of academia without a job. Hawkins had made an impression at GRiD, however, and they asked him back to help create some new ideas.

And that's what he did: His first product, in 1989, was the GRiDPAD, a portable pen-based computer (in the very early days of bulky laptops) that could read the handwriting that you scrawled on the screen. The problem was not just the GRiDPAD's propensity for turning your scrawl into meaningless prose; it was also expensive (more than $2,000), had a short battery life, and was, while portable, too heavy to carry around at all times.

Sensing that the GRiDPAD was not going to succeed, Hawkins designed the specs for an improved handheld called Zoomer. Zoomer flopped for essentially the same reasons: It was heavy, expensive, and slow. Even worse, it appeared shortly after Apple's humiliating failure with its first tablet computer, the infamous Newton. Hawkins tried to rally the troops for another go with Zoomer 2, but no one was interested. In the opinion of investors and the press, portable pen computing was finished. But Hawkins didn't think so.

With Zoomer out of the picture, Hawkins went back home and pondered the reason for the failure of the handhelds. Eventually he realized that while he and the rest of the handheld loyalists were trying to add features to the product—long battery life, multiple apps, connectivity with desktops, even e-mail (which had barely begun)—they were missing the gorilla in their midst: What people wanted was not an all-inclusive device, but a handy, inexpensive machine that would deliver a *reasonable* number of features. They didn't want a miniature computer—simply a device that *interfaced* with one.

With this epiphany, Hawkins went into his garage and pulled a piece of scrap lumber from a box in the corner. He ran it through a jigsaw that stood nearby. After a few cuts and some sanding, he had a tablet small enough to slip into a shirt pocket. He made a paper facing for this slab of wood, with a screen and some function keys, and he was done.

Hawkins walked around with his wooden prototype for several weeks. If you had spied him on the street, you might have seen him stop suddenly, as if struck with an idea, pull out the piece of wood, perhaps punch a few of the buttons, then slip it back into his pocket. He had a "pen" to write on the screen as well—actually, it was a chopstick that he had whittled down to size.

"I just walked around, imagining what I might use it for," he said as we stood there in his garage, staring at the little jigsaw he'd used to cut that important piece of wood. The PalmPilot, as it was called, debuted in the spring of 1996 and changed not only pen computing but the entire personal computer industry.

As the Hawkins example suggests, visionaries don't succeed by lying in bed with their dreams floating idly above their heads. They get out into the world and *experience* things, and from that, shape their ideas. As the anatomist William Harvey said, "I profess to learn and teach anatomy not from books, but from dissections, not from the tenets of philosophers, but from the fabric of nature."[22] The Wright brothers, too, learned through tactile experience. "They had a particularly acute sense of materials," says Peter Jakab in *Visions of a Flying Machine,* noting that the brothers had "a highly developed sensuous affinity for machines."[23] One can imagine Hawkins shaping his slab of wood into a PalmPilot, or Harvey cutting into a corpse to reveal its heart, or the Wright brothers shaping white-pine spars and fabric into a flier. As Berkeley philosophy professor Alva Noe notes, "Seeing is not something that happens to us . . . it is something we do."[24]

That's why Steve Jobs was so eager to peek inside Xerox's Palo Alto Research Center in 1979. Jobs had already heard about the "graphical user interface" and the "mouse" that PARC's engineers had designed. Rumors about them had swirled for quite some time in the closely knit Silicon Valley community. But what Jobs wanted was to *see* these advances with his own eyes, to study them from every angle he could. Even when he did, it still took Jobs and his team five more years of engineering to bring what they saw at PARC to market in Apple's Lisa and Mac computers.[25]

Sadly, the practice of getting out and seeing something firsthand has been in decline in American engineering. "Until the 1960s," writes technology historian Eugene Ferguson in *Engineering and the Mind's Eye,* "a student in an American engineering school was expected to use his mind's eye to examine things that engineers had designed—to 'look' at them, listen to them, walk around them, and thus develop an intuitive 'feel' for the way the material world works."[26]

But since then, Ferguson says, visual training has been replaced by a blind reliance on data and mathematics. In a 1980s survey of engineering schools worldwide, researchers found that most American engineering programs had dropped their required courses in engineering design. Where do they still survive? In Japan.[27]

The same decline in visualization has been seen in mathematics. In 1614, Scotsman John Napier created the idea of the logarithm, which is considered a "visual" mathematical technique. Napierian logarithms allowed engineers to *visualize* their calculations in ways that they could not with numbers alone, notes Ferguson. How? Because logarithmic scales represented numbers by their distance along a straight line: Using a slide rule, engineers can visually see—they can acquire a "sense of reasonableness" in the final computation (this is not the case when one computes using a computer or calculator). It was this method, along with Cartesian coordinate geometry—which also uses visual images to clarify relationships among abstract concepts—that allowed engineers to build the marvels of the industrial age. "The advantages of graphical statics," notes Ferguson, "is that it gives a sense of what's going on—a feel—permitting the engineer to build in the mind's eye a vision of the forces in a complex structure." With these the engineer can stand back and ask: Does it *feel* right? Does it *look* right?[28]

Fortunately, the tide is turning. American schools are realizing that running one's hand across the materials and walking around structures to gain perspective are not poor substitutes for computer simulations and elaborate mathematical formulas. They're practical steps in learning to see.

You wouldn't need to tell the Nobel Prize–winning physicist Richard Feynman what ideas can come to mind out of simply walking around. Once when he was in the cafeteria at Cornell University, he noticed a student tossing a plate above his head. "As the plate went up in the air I saw it wobble, and I noticed the red medallion of Cornell on the plate going around," he notes in his memoir *Surely You're Joking, Mr. Feynman!* "It was pretty obvious to me that the medallion went around faster than the wobbling." That random observation kicked off a chain of thought in Feynman's head. Pretty soon he was calculating wobble rates, which led to thoughts about electron orbits. Before long that segued into quantum electrodynamics. And in the end, "The diagrams and the whole business that I got the Nobel Prize for came from that piddling around with the wobbling plate," he confessed. Such is the prize for keeping your eyes wide open.[29]

Steve Jobs admits to few idols. But one is Edwin Land, the college dropout who invented the polarizing filters used in everything from car headlights to sunglasses. Land, of course, also invented the Polaroid Land Camera. It happened like this: One time when Land and his three-year-old daughter were in New Mexico, she asked why she couldn't immediately see a photograph that he had snapped. He took a short walk through the desert, pondering that question. By the time he had returned (and it was no more than an hour, he recalled), he had visualized the elements of the instant camera. "You always start with a fantasy," he said. "Part of the fantasy technique is to visualize something as perfect. Then with experiments you work back from the fantasy to reality, hacking away at the components."[30]

Now, some 40 years later, Land had agreed to meet with Jobs at Land's laboratory in Cambridge, Massachusetts. Jobs was on one side of the conference table, Land on the other. They were of different generations, but cut from similar cloth: Jobs, the dropout from Reed College; Land, the dropout from Harvard. Jobs, working nights inventing video games at Atari; Land, lifting a window and sneaking into a lab at Columbia University at night to use the school's equipment. Jobs, neglecting his clothes and his health to build his PCs. Land, who in his prime worked 20 hours a day, forgetting to eat, and wearing the same clothes for days on end.

Land once told a reporter, "If anything is worth doing, it's worth doing to excess . . . My whole life has been spent trying to teach people that intense concentration for hour after hour can bring out in people resources they didn't know they had." Similarly, Jobs had once remarked, "We have a short period of time on this earth . . . My feeling is that I've got to accomplish a lot of things while I'm young."[31]

Now the two visionaries were in the same room for the first time. Apple CEO John Sculley sat to the side and watched. Sculley later wrote in his autobiography that neither Jobs nor Land looked at each other as they spoke about their dreams and inventions, but stared at something between them in the center of the table.[32]

"I could see what the Polaroid camera should be," Land remarked. "It was just as real to me as if it were sitting in front of me before I had ever built one." As the two focused on the emptiness between them, the Land camera came into focus, like a hologram.

Jobs watched. His eyes were focused as well. "Yeah, that's exactly the way I saw the Macintosh," he said.

Later, when driving home, Jobs told Sculley, "It's like when I walk into a room and I want to talk about a product that hasn't been invented yet. I can see the product as if it's sitting there right in the center of the table. It's like what I've got to do is materialize it and bring it to life—harvest it just like Dr. Land said."[33]

Sculley drove on, stunned. "Both of them had this ability to—well, not invent products, but discover products," he wrote later. "Both of them said these products have always existed, it's just that no one had ever seen them before. We were the ones who discovered them."

CHAPTER FOUR

Intuition

When Steve Jobs pulled his black Mercedes to the curb in front of his boyhood home, he sat in the car for a good ten minutes, speaking heatedly into his car phone. As I mentioned earlier, I could hear the word "Pixar" spilling from the partly opened window.

I knew that Steve Jobs had been booted out of his own company—tossed out by John Sculley ten years earlier in 1985. But Pixar didn't make much of an impression on me. I knew it had something to do with a cartoon movie, *Toy Story*, which was premiering in a few weeks. But that was it.

Jobs climbed out of his car and strode toward us. By us I mean Brent Schlender and me. Brent was the tropical-shirt-wearing, saxophone-playing Silicon Valley correspondent for *Fortune*. He was a well-connected and well-liked personality in Silicon Valley. Jobs, in his usual intense way, shook Brent's hand. Brent introduced me, and Jobs gave me a quick handshake. He turned quickly back to Brent. Jobs knew that Brent knew what was going on at Apple—and he wanted to know, too.

As I listened to Jobs interrogate Brent, it reminded me of the guy who had been dumped by the girl. He didn't want you to know he still cared for her, but he desperately wanted to know what she'd been up to. Poor guy, I thought, he really misses Apple. But that ship's gone, baby. There are no second acts in this life. Or so I thought.[1]

What happened shortly thereafter, of course, was that Jobs *did* get back into Apple. CEO Gil Amelio—who had succeeded Michael Spindler at Apple, who had succeeded John Sculley, who had dumped Jobs in 1985—was now out himself. Apple had suffered a $1.6 billion loss during Amelio's 18 months at the helm, and its market share had dwindled to 3 percent from 10 percent. Now Jobs, like Odysseus in the Homeric saga, had returned.

On his first day back at Apple, Jobs strolled into the conference room. He was wearing shorts, sneakers, and a few days of chin stubble. Jobs dropped into a chair and slowly spun around. "Okay, tell me what's wrong with this place," he said to the assembled group. After some mumbled replies, Jobs cut them off. "It's the products," he exclaimed. "The products suck! There's no sex in them anymore."[2]

For Steve Jobs, that was a pretty predictable outburst. But what happened in the following few weeks was not. With uncharacteristic coolness and calm Jobs combed through the entire company, meeting with every department, and quickly—because Apple was only a few months away from bankruptcy—narrowed the focus of the firm.

Under Sculley and Spindler, Apple had initiated hundreds of projects. Amelio had killed about 300 of them. But that left 50—with some real sacred cows among them, including the Newton handheld computer and a promising line of laser printers. Within weeks Jobs had narrowed the major initiates to 10. Gone were the laser printers, gone was the Newton. Gone were cherished software projects as well.[3]

Jobs stepped up to a whiteboard and drew a simple two-by-two line grid. Across the top he wrote "consumer" and "professional." Down the side he wrote "portable" and "desktop." Jobs filled the grid's four empty slots with *four* Apple computers. Just four products—two notebooks and two desktops.[4]

How in the world did he whittle ten products down to four?

Jobs consulted with the various departments at Apple. They offered their suggestions. Jobs also consulted his friends in the industry. They probably had strong opinions and aired them. But when it got down to the nitty-gritty—when Jobs was left by himself staring out the window—the decision was his alone. No one was going to tell Steve Jobs what to do. So how did he make this final, up-against-the-wall, it's-this-or-bankruptcy call? I think I know.

I think it happened the same way that the quantum physicist Richard Feynman was able to scan several pages of complex math formulas and casually conclude, "Looks about right."[5]

The same way that Richard Branson—on the way to the loo—scanned a pub napkin upon which a freelance designer had scrawled the now-iconic Virgin logo, and remarked, "That'll do."[6]

The same way that Walt Disney decided, after a short rumination, that the world's first full-length feature cartoon would not be *Gulliver's Travels* (which Douglas Fairbanks suggested), nor *Alice in Wonderland* (which Mary Pickford was pushing for), and not even *The Iliad* (cartoonist James Thurber liked that one), but a fairy tale by the Brothers Grimm, featuring a cast of seven dwarfs initially named Scrappy, Cranky, Dirty, Awful, Blabby, Silly, and Daffy.[7]

In short, they went with their gut.

In the field of neuroscience, going with your gut is called intuition. What is intuition? It has been called "unconscious intelligence" by some psychologists, the "adaptive unconscious" by others.

To understand intuition you have to understand that we're really of two minds. First there's the conscious mind. It makes lists, recalls conversations, rehashes events. In one remarkable study, a researcher dispensed beepers to nearly 2,000 people. When the device beeped, he asked them to jot down precisely what was going on in their heads. The results revealed that humanity is not humming with higher-order thought. One of the participants found herself repeating "Twinkies; granola" for most of the day. Another ruminated about the decorations she would use for an upcoming Christmas party, A third, a young doctor, was caught scooping her cat box. "Just a quick cleaning up," her inner monologue revealed.[8]

Francis Galton, the Victorian intellectual who studied the powers of visual recall, also wondered how many thoughts pop into one's mind during any given amount of time. To find out, he decided to count the number of thoughts he had as he walked a few hundred yards down the Pall Mall in London. He noted that it took exactly "660 seconds to form 505 ideas; that is about the rate of 50 in a minute or 3,000 in an hour." But many of them were repetitive ideas, he confessed, noting that many "seemed to be something like actors in theatres, when large processions are represented who march off one side of the stage, and, going round by the back, come again at the other." Not only were there a lot of ideas marching through, but few of them were particularly unique. "The general impression they have left upon me is like that which many of us have experienced," he wrote in his journal, "when the basement of our house happens to be under thorough sanitary repairs, and we realize for the first time the complex system of drains and gas and water pipes, flues, bell-wiring and so forth, upon which our comfort depends, but which are usually hidden out of sight, and of whose existence, so long as they acted well, we had never troubled ourselves."[9]

We sometimes have real, substantive thoughts. But that's generally not the stuff of everyday consciousness. Most of our *conscious* thinking, as Galton revealed, is enormously mundane.

But then there's the *subconscious*. Though we aren't aware of it, there's a lot of decision making going on down there. Muscles, joints, and skin are signaling the orientation of our body, keeping us positioned and preventing us from falling down. The hypothalamus is regulating the level of blood sugar. Modulator neurons are distributing dopamine, norepinephrine, serotonin, acetylcholine, and other neurotransmitters to the cerebral cortex and subcortical nuclei.[10]

Every part of the body is sending and receiving information to and from the brain. Even our skin is aware of its surroundings; when experimenters hooked video cameras to the skin of blindfolded participants, they found that they could discern shapes through the sensations communicated through the skin.[11] And if that isn't enough, the whole body is synchronized to the tune of the suprachiasmatic nuclei, a pair of ganglia the size of a grain of rice that act like an internal clock. There may be hundreds of timers in the body, in fact, pulsating busily, filling the subconscious brain with a blend of rhythms.[12]

Descending even deeper reveals another busy world of intelligence. "On the surface of the cell we would see millions of openings, like the portholes of a vast space ship, opening and closing to allow a continuing stream of material to flow in and out," explains Dr. James Le Fanu in *The Rise and Fall of Modern Medicine*. If we were to enter one of these openings, he writes, "we would see endless corridors branching in every direction away from the perimeter of the cell, some leading to the central memory bank in the nucleus and others to assembly plant units. The nucleus itself would be a vast spherical dome inside of which we would see, all neatly stacked together, the miles of coiled chains of the DNA molecules. A huge range of products and raw materials would shuffle along the corridors in a highly ordered fashion to and from all the various assembly plants in the outer regions of the cell."

It's a fascinating view of the subconscious world, one that would have stunned any of the pioneers of medicine. Le Fanu continued: "We would see that nearly every feature of our advanced machines has its analogue in the cell," he continues. "Artificial languages and their decoding systems, memory banks for information storage and retrieval, elegant control systems regulating the automated assembly of parts and components, proof-reading devices utilised for quality control, assembly processes involving the principle of pre-fabrication and modular construction. What we would be witnessing would be an object resembling an immense automated factory carrying out almost as many unique functions as all the manufacturing activities of man on Earth."[13]

So down below we've got some serious business going on—and upstairs we're worrying about the cat box. Yet when we think about ourselves, we think of the conscious mind as the commander in chief. It's the conscious mind that makes decisions and weighs life's choices. So it's natural that we think of this brain area and its functions as the command post.

But lately, neuroscientists are questioning that interpretation. It has been estimated that the body can absorb millions of pieces of information a second. The conscious mind, experiments have shown, can process only about 40 a second.[14] That's why many researchers say the information-processing ability of the subconscious plays a bigger part in our lives than it has traditionally been given credit for.

Philosopher Dan Dennett argues that the subconscious mind is really "the President" of our beings. In other words, the subconscious is what gives us our orders. What, then, is the conscious mind? "The Press Secretary," he replies.[15] The subconscious mind calls the shots, and the conscious mind simply announces a few of those executive decisions to the conscious brain, he says. Agreeing with Dennett is psychologist Timothy Wilson, author of *Strangers to Ourselves*. "The adaptive unconscious plays a major executive role in our mental lives," he notes. "It gathers information, interprets and evaluates it, and sets goals in motion, quickly and efficiently."[16]

Just as the conscious mind is always hunting patterns, then, so is the subconscious mind. We just don't realize it. Have you ever had that certain *feeling*? Something just doesn't seem right. You know it in your gut, no matter how hard your analytical mind tries to dismiss it.

Life's events are often random: Without notice, stock markets crash, volcanoes explode, cars speed through stop signs and kill innocent victims. But if life were not in most ways *predictable* (we plant an apple seed and get an apple tree, not an armadillo), we never would have survived. For that reason, the brain is always looking for familiar patterns. They're our key to survival.

But very often—with our heads in the litter box, or worse still, absorbed in office politics—we aren't watching. Fortunately, our subconscious is. It's collecting clues, and, without our knowing, connecting the dots to see the patterns that count.

Take speech. After a lunch with friends, we leave with the sense of having participated in a fluid, articulate conversation. But have you ever looked at the transcript of a casual conversation?

At the *Wall Street Journal* I once covered a bribery trial. The FBI had wired up an informant with a tape recorder and sent him into an Italian restaurant with several of the suspects. When I read the subsequent transcript, I was surprised at (in addition to the fact that everyone was named Frankie) how disjointed the conversation really was. I came away realizing that we really speak in fragments. We hardly ever complete a thought—and this is particularly so when we are in a spirited conversation. That's why most journalists learn not to tape interviews in restaurants, and particularly in bars: The results are almost unintelligible.

The playwright David Mamet brilliantly captures the disjointed pattern of everyday speech in this snippet from *Glengarry Glen Ross:*[17]

Moss: It's too . . .

Aaronow: It is.

Moss: Eh?

Aaronow: It's too . . .

Moss: You get a bad month, all of a . . .

Aaronow: You're on this . . .

Moss: All of, they got you on this "board . . ."

Aaronow: I, I . . . I . . .

Moss: Some *contest* board . . .

Aaronow: I . . .

Moss: It's not right.

Aaronow: It's not.

Moss: No. *(Pause.)*

With thought fragments parading as communication, how do we understand one another? Not to worry—the subconscious picks up the patterns and makes the best of them. The subconscious on both sides agrees to what has been left unsaid.[18] And it all happens without us being aware of it at all.

In fact, our subconscious not only translates language for us, it even interprets body language from the speakers around us. In the 1960s researcher William Condon made a 4.5-second film clip of a woman speaking at a dinner table. She gazes across at a boy and man sitting there and says affably, "You all should come around every night. We never have had a dinnertime like this in months." Condon then broke the 4.5-second segment into individual frames, each representing 1/45th of a second. As he studied the film he began to realize that the people at the table were communicating as much by their minute body motions as they were by speech alone.

Eyebrows lifted, eyelashes fluttered, hands moved, shoulders tilted, all in a herky-jerky manner. It was a dance, like honeybees communicating by dancing in the hive—micromovements that Condon termed "interactional synchrony."[19] Once again, without our knowledge, the subconscious is interpreting the patterns of the world for us.

Can your subconscious predict the future? A few years ago a research team brought together participants in a lab at Case Western Reserve University. The participants were seated before a screen. When the lights were lowered, they were told, they would see a spot of light flashing randomly across the screen. All they had to do was shift their gaze as quickly as possible from one flash of light to the next.

As the experiment continued, a strange thing happened: Their eyes took about a fifth of a second to respond to a new light, and another fifth of a second to rotate to the new position. Spookily, they began to anticipate where the spot of light would appear next. After 30 minutes of practice, their eyes were snapping on some of the targets *before* the light went on. What kind of intuitive magic was this? Even though the lights followed a complex predictable pattern, the subjects hadn't a clue.[20]

A similar phenomenon was seen a few years ago off the tip of South Africa, when nature photographer Simon King was sent by the BBC to film the run of some 60,000 Cape fur seals and their pups across a body of choppy seas with great white sharks roaming beneath the surface. When a shark took a bead on a seal, it would rush to the surface with enormous power—breaching the surface and sending itself, with a seal in its teeth, 20 feet or more into the air. To capture the shot, King strapped himself to the back of the boat. On his shoulder he carried a special camera used by researchers to photograph simulated car crashes in ultraslow motion.

The sea was wide and choppy and the shark attacks seemingly

random. A shark would come boiling out of the sea at one spot, then from another 50 feet away. And sometimes hours would go by without a single shark attack at all. Making matters worse, the footage had to be downloaded to a hard drive between each shot to make room for the next. As one shot was being processed for a possible hit, King was left without a camera as other shark hits happened around him.

Yet the pictures that King got—appearing in the phenomenal series *Planet Earth: Shallow Seas*—were spectacular. We see the sea bursting open from below, with the limp body of a seal lifted skyward by a hungry shark.

How could King have captured that? He could have aimed the camera steadfastly at one patch of water and hoped for the best. Or he could have swung the camera continuously from spot to spot. But how could he get those shots that chronicled the attack from the time the water was undisturbed to the moment it erupted in an upward-bound shark-seal projectile? How in the world could he predict where and when the attack would occur?

For the first two weeks of shooting, King came up empty-handed. But gradually he "began to understand the randomness of the attacks," explained the narrator of *Planet Earth*.[21] Somehow, and very intuitively, King began to point his camera in the right place, anticipating the strike of the shark.

This was the same phenomenon seen in the previous Case Western Reserve study. In that experiment, the researchers had embedded a pattern sequence—1-5-3-1-4—within other random sequences. The subjects were not consciously aware of the regularity of the sequence, but the subconscious was—and led the subjects to snap their eyes to the right targets on the screen.

In an even more revealing study, participants were asked to press buttons labeled 1, 2, or 3 as soon as they saw the corresponding number appear on a computer screen. As before, the sequence followed patterns, but patterns so complex the participants didn't consciously recognize them. But this time the researchers were mapping the flow of blood within the brains of the participants with a positron emission tomography (PET) machine. And what they discovered was remarkable: As the patterns changed, the brain's premotor area—the left anterior cingulate cortex and right ventral striatum—took notice. Even though the patients were completely unaware of it, their subconscious minds were figuring out the patterns.[22]

Neuroscientist Antonio Damasio demonstrated the power of the subconscious through a simple card game. In this case, the participants were wired up to polygraphs. They selected cards from one of four decks. Each card offered either a cash reward or a penalty. The goal was to finish the game with more money than anyone else. Unbeknownst to the participants, two of the four decks were stacked with big cash prizes as well as big penalties. The two other decks offered smaller rewards and smaller penalties.

The players plunged in, each in turn selecting a card. Meanwhile, the researchers monitored the wavering needles of the polygraph machines. In the early rounds of the game, the needles lay flat. But after several rounds, a strange thing began to happen: Each time a player reached for one of the "riskier" decks, a hand hovering over the pile, the needle jumped. Though the conscious mind hadn't caught on to the difference between the decks, the player's autonomic nervous system "winced"—secreting tiny amounts of sweat that raised the skin's resistance to the electrical current.

The players continued to draw from the big–reward/penalty decks. But gradually, apparently heeding signs being sent down from the amygdalae, stopped altogether, drawing entirely from the low-risk decks instead.

"There was no way for the players to carry out a precise calculation of gains and losses," Damasio noted in *Descartes' Error.*

"However, bit by bit, they developed a hunch that some decks—namely A and B—are more 'dangerous' than others." Intuition had intervened.[23]

While the subconscious draws on patterns that we are not consciously aware of, it also pulls from another source that is in many ways richer and more grounded than the rational mind: the emotional mind.

This source has been called "emotional intelligence." The term was coined by Peter Salovey of Yale University and John D. Mayer of the University of New Hampshire in the early 1990s. "Emotional intelligence," they explained, "involves the ability to perceive accurately, appraise, and express emotion; the ability to access and/or generate feelings when they facilitate thought; the ability to understand emotion and emotional knowledge; and the ability to regulate emotions to promote emotional and intellectual growth."[24]

Salovey and Mayer made their discoveries in the late 1980s and early 1990s, and shortly thereafter the idea of emotional intelligence swept into the public consciousness through the best-selling book *Emotional Intelligence,* by Daniel Goleman. In it, Goleman explained that emotional intelligence, which includes self-awareness, self-discipline, and empathy, can add up to a different way of being smart, one that can trump pure analytical IQ as one continues through life. *Emotional Intelligence* was an epiphany, particularly because it helped explain why some many people who got straight Cs in school end up later in life at the top of the heap.

So what is the source of emotional intelligence? The emotional mind seems to arise to a great extent from the amygdalae, twin clusters of neurons, each the size and shape of an almond, buried deep in the brain. Patients without functioning amygdalae can be productive, functioning, even somewhat social, but they are emotionally flat. They can look at pictures of a horrific car crash without a reaction, as though ice water is running through their veins. (The power of this simile would be lost on the reader without an amygdala.)

The emotional amygdala, however, did not evolve to help you spot similes, feel compassion, or even win poetry contests. It is a survival tool. When you glance down a wooded path and see a coiled object, the image doesn't go first to your neocortex for rational logic sequencing: *If* that coiled object has a flickering tongue, *and if* that coiled shape also has a diamond-shaped head, *then* . . . Rather, the signal goes from your eye to the thalamus and then directly to the amygdalae, where all hell breaks loose. You leap out of the way.

In *Emotional Intelligence,* Goleman recalls jumping out of bed when a pile of boxes suddenly collapsed in his closet. The crash in the night went straight to his amygdalae, he noted, and only milliseconds later, when it reached his neocortex, did he have the opportunity to collect his wits and figure out what had happened.[25] This is our basic survival instinct at work, and it is as hardwired into humans as it is in any other species.

Emotional intelligence is not only a guide in avoiding physical hazards; it's a moral compass. In a *New York Times* op-ed, David Brooks argued that the American legal system is "based on a useful falsehood . . . that this is a nation of laws, not men; that in rendering decisions, objective judges are able to put aside emotion and unruly passions and issue options on the basis of pure reason." He adds, "Most people know this is untrue. In reality decisions are made by perfect minds in ambiguous circumstances."

So what counts, then? Brooks chooses emotions. "Emotions are the processes we use to assign value to different possibilities," he notes. "Emotions move us toward things and ideas that produce pleasure and away from things and ideas that produce pain . . .

People without emotions cannot make sensible decisions because they don't know how much anything is worth."[26]

What's surprising about the subconscious is that it not only makes decisions for us, but often prefers less information than more. In an era when data mining has been heralded as the future of decision making, it comes as a surprise that the mind often thinks best with less. But it does. People frequently make better decisions with less information.

Recently, psychologist Gerd Gigerenzer and economist Andreas Ortmann entered a stock-picking contest sponsored by *Capital*, an investment magazine. In the contest, *Capital*'s editor chose fifty international Internet stocks, any one of which could be bought, sold, or held in any manner for six weeks.

Ten thousand participants, most of them seasoned traders, threw their hats into the ring. But, as Gigerenzer tells it, only one group really stood out: his own. Rather than base their trading on any kind of research or industry insight, Gigerenzer and Ortmann randomly asked 100 citizens of Berlin, people they stopped on the street, to pick ten stocks that they recognized from a field of fifty. In the end, Gigerenzer's group not only topped more than 88 percent of the other contestants, but (in making a gain of 2.5 percent) beat the editor-in-chief's portfolio, which lost 18.5 percent.

Gigerenzer was so impressed by the results that he rounded up a group of people who had very little interest in the stock market. They chose another portfolio—and he invested $50,000 in it. After six months he had gained 47 percent on his investment—more, he noted, than the market itself and even higher than mutual funds that were managed by the pros.[27]

That a certain level of ignorance is bliss has been proven out in other studies. In one case, college counselors were given transcripts, test scores, application essays, and other data about students and asked to predict their freshman-year grades. They were even allowed to interview the applicants. Competing against them was a mathematical formula based solely on two pieces of information—high school grade-point average and the score on a single standardized test. Which method better predicted the success of the applicant? As it turned out, the assessments based on the mathematical formula were slightly superior to those made with a great deal more information.[28]

In another study, psychologist Ap Dijksterhuis and his colleagues at the University of Amsterdam asked the participants to evaluate four hypothetical cars. When he asked the participants to choose the best car (one was superior) based on four attributes (such as legroom or trunk space), the participants handily picked the right one. But when Dijksterhuis gave them *more* information—in this case, twelve attributes—the participants had a much harder time doing so. The real clincher to this case, however, is that the participants who were given the opportunity to ponder the twelve attributes did more poorly than the participants who were asked to choose without the opportunity to ponder their choice. In other words, the participants who listened to the twelve attributes and then had to choose quickly—and, hence, *intuitively*—actually made better choices. In another study, Dijksterhuis found that shoppers at an IKEA furniture store who spent a lot of time pondering their purchases were, days later, less satisfied with them than people who had made snap decisions. Once again, *more* information was not able to produce better results than a few good facts.

Dijksterhuis noted that when people were buying simple things—"like shampoos and oven gloves"—they were happier having consciously pondered the purchase. "But once the decision was more complex, such as for a house, too much thinking about it led people to make the wrong choice," he said. His conclusion: "At some point in our evolution we started to make decisions consciously—and we're not very good at it. We should learn to let our unconscious handle the complicated things."[29]

In any number of experiments, the power of "limited knowledge" has been revealed.

In one study by Nalini Ambady and Robert Rosenthal, participants were shown six-second (silent) video clips of professors lecturing. Was a particular professor successful or not? Based on this scant, six seconds of evidence, the participants were still able to separate the best teachers (that received the highest student evaluations) from the poor ones—again, based on a scant, six-second sample![30]

In a similar study, psychologist Paul Slovic had horse-racing bookmakers select 5 pieces of information that they had previously found useful (from a list of 88 that included the jockey's weight and the horse's previous performance), and asked them to predict the outcome of races based on those 5 items. Subsequently the bookmakers were asked to pick *10 more* pieces of information—and predict again. Slovic found that regardless of whether they had 5 pieces of information or 40, the bookmakers' predictions didn't improve. But their *confidence* did: from a 20 percent confidence level with 5 pieces of information to 30 percent with 40 pieces of information.[31]

What does this tell us? When making forecasts, says Gerd Gigerenzer, "one good reason" works better than a lot of data. In fact, he notes, the only use for complex analysis is in explaining the past.[32] For example, reams of data and regulatory inspections did not predict the 2010 BP oil spill in the Gulf of Mexico with any clarity—otherwise changes would have been made. But in looking *back* to that rig explosion and subsequent spill, investigators will benefit from all the data that they can collect. Data explain only the past, not the future, many scientists believe. And the past, as they say, is no guarantee of future performance!

Notes Nassim Taleb, "The more information you give someone, the more hypotheses they will formulate along the way, and the worse off they will be . . . Additional knowledge of the minutiae of daily business can be useless, even toxic."[33] Perhaps the reason that we can remember only a few things before forgetting, then, is that the brain is protecting us. It understands that too much knowledge is a dangerous thing.

So intuition is essential to the visionary. Visionaries *almost always* work at the edge of our understanding, where information is scarce or nonexistent and where intuitive decisions are often the only choice.

Little wonder, then, that Steve Jobs didn't waste time with focus groups and research before choosing four computers for the future of Apple. Nor did Richard Branson agonize over entering the airline business. In fact, Branson made his decision entirely on his gut reaction to the idea—and a phone call to Boeing in Seattle to determine if they had a spare 747 for lease. In his autobiography, he writes that in general he relies "far more on gut instinct than researching huge amounts of statistics," and that he usually makes up his mind about a business proposal "within thirty seconds—and on whether it excites me."[34]

Branson's friends think his behavior is insane. When he made that phone call to Boeing to start an airline, this was certainly the case. "I think they realized I had done all the market research that I felt I needed to do and had made up my mind," Branson notes in his autobiography. He continues, " 'You're a maniac,' Simon Draper said to me. 'We've been friends since we were teenagers, but I'm not sure we can carry on working together. What I'm telling you is that you can go ahead with this over my dead body.' " Branson *did* start his airline, and Draper, with a live body, not a dead one, went along for the ride.[35]

The power of intuition has been celebrated in such books as Malcolm Gladwell's best-selling *Blink*: Listen to your inner voice and go with the flow, we are told. It all sounds great. But not everyone is convinced. In fact, some critics warn that intuition is far from infallible.

CalTech physicist Leonard Mlodinow notes in his best seller *The Drunkard's Walk* that intuitive thinking, based on pattern recognition, often suggests precisely the *wrong* way to go. "We often employ intuitive processes when we make assessments and choices in uncertain situations," he writes. "Those processes no doubt carried an evolutionary advantage when we had to decide whether a saber-toothed tiger was smiling because it was fat and happy or because it was famished and saw us as its next meal. But the modern world has a different balance, and today those intuitive processes come with drawbacks."[36]

Suppose you have a deck of red and green cards, Mlodinow continues. You draw a few cards and are asked to predict the next. If there is a pattern, and you can consciously or unconsciously detect it, you'll be right. But suppose the cards are randomly stacked? Then your intuition will *not* help. Moreover, if you are competing in this experiment against a laboratory rat (which is choosing at random against your pseudointuitive pattern), the rat will win.

"Intuition tells us that we pay attention to more than we do, that our memories are more detailed and robust than they are, that confident people are competent people, that we know more than we really do, that coincidences and correlations demonstrate causation, and that our brains have vast reserves of power that are easy to unlock," note Chabris and Simons in *The Invisible Gorilla*. "But in all these cases, our intuitions are wrong, and they can cost us our fortunes, our health, and even our lives if we follow them blindly."[37] Before we praise our intuition for having us leap away from what at first appears to be a coiled rope, we have to recognize that our intuition may have been wrong, and that what lies in our path *is* a coiled rope. Meanwhile, we have just leapt off the face of a cliff.

Let's leave it at this, then: Intuition is a judgment call. Visionaries who survive have come to know when their intuition is on the mark. Intuition favors the prepared mind, like the surgeon who is skilled at a particular procedure and has done lots of them. That seems to be the balance that visionaries achieve as well—practiced insight, leavened with intuition.

The visionary is a pattern hunter. And as the patterns begin to take shape, the visionary paces the hall anxiously, staring out the window. The cognitive dissonance builds between what is and what will be. The visionary's sense of discomfort grows.

At some point when the thinker, exhausted, has stopped concentrating on the problem at hand, the brain slips into that single-mind immersion that Hungarian psychologist Mihaly Csikszentmihalyi famously termed the state of "flow." Whereas we spend most of our lives thinking about the past and the future, the flow puts us into that narrow shaft of time called the present. It's a place the brain doesn't take us to very often.

MRIs show that, in the state of flow, the brain is quieting down. The flickering of activity recedes into weak flashes of color. The thinker, at this point, is probably aware of nothing at all. Whether it is intuition, or visualization, or the dawning of an awakening that draws the visionary near, at last the time of inspiration arrives. This is the famous Eureka! moment.

Steve Jobs "stood back": "You can't really predict what will happen," he said. "But you can feel the direction you're going. And that's about as close as you can get. Then you just stand back and get out of the way, and these things take on a life of their own."[38]

John Lennon just took a nap: "I'd spent five hours that morning trying to write a song that was meaningful and good. I was just sitting, trying to think, and I thought of myself sitting there doing nothing and going nowhere. Once I'd thought of that, it was easy; it all came out. No, I remember now, I'd actually *stopped* trying to think of something. Nothing would come. I was cheesed off and went for a lie down, having given up. Then I thought of myself as nowhere man, sitting in this nowhere land. 'Nowhere Man' came, words and music, the whole damn thing. The same with 'In My Life.' I'd struggled for days and hours, trying to write clever lyrics. Then I gave up, and 'In My Life' came to me. Letting it go is the whole game."[39]

Einstein closed his eyes and let his fingers wander over the piano keys. Then he jumped up. "There, now I've got it!" his sister Maja remembers him exclaiming as he hurried off into his study.[40]

That moment when the new pattern snaps into place has been described many ways: like scales falling from the eyes, like a flash of lightning, like molecules of water bouncing randomly around and, upon reaching a freezing temperature, snapping instantly into rigid lines. Something new comes across your consciousness. It "dawns" on you. Says physicist Carlo Rubbia, "It's an irrational and an instinctive moment in which something clicks in your mind and you say, 'Why don't we do this—I mean, why *not?*' "[41]

The snapping of fingers perfectly describes the moment of inspiration (and makes you wonder if the opposable thumb was actually made for this purpose). For it is two *opposing* forces—what *is* and what *should be*—that are being resolved.

It is surprising how something as portentous as an epiphany resembles the punch line of a joke: "Does your dog bite?" Inspector Clouseau of *The Pink Panther* fame asks the hotel clerk as he sees a dog at his feet. "No," the clerk responds. Clouseau bends over to pet the dog and has his sleeve ripped off. "I thought you said your dog doesn't bite!" he remarks angrily. Replies the clerk, "That's not my dog."

We laugh at such jokes because the pattern change is unexpected. It comes out of the blue. "The punch line," according to Horace Judson, former professor of the history of science at Johns Hopkins University, "tells us that a set of things that we thought belonged to one pattern was really, all along, making another pattern."[42]

Incredible as it seems, the brain's search for a resolution to dissonance is exactly what you might hear in a comedy club: When the U.S. Postal Service can't deliver the mail overnight, we get . . . (laughter growing) FedEx! When the Internet has billions of pages of text that are impossible to search, we get (chortles and applause) Google! When we can't get a good cup of brewed coffee, we get (drum roll and rim shot) Starbucks!

The counterintuitive thought in all of this is that for an idea to really be radical, it has to be in some way ridiculous. "First of all you have to take it as a joke," explains Carlo Rubbia. "Any fundamental advances in our field are made by looking at it with the smile of a child who plays a game."[43]

Science writer Isaac Asimov said, "The most exciting phrase to hear in science, the one that heralds the most discoveries, is not Eureka! (I found it!) but, 'That's funny . . .' "[44] That phenomenon was also noticed by Lewis Thomas, the former dean of medicine at Yale and president of Memorial Sloan-Kettering Institute. "It seems to me that whenever I have been around a laboratory at a time when something very interesting has happened, it has at first seemed to be quite funny," he recalled. "There's laughter connected with the surprise—it does look funny. And whenever you hear laughter and somebody saying, 'But that's preposterous!'—you can tell that things are going well and that something probably worth looking at has begun to happen in the lab."[45]

Indeed, this is the secret of visionary ideas: Most earthshaking ideas look *funny* at first. They are not *sensible*. Think of the jokes that have been pulled: Jobs introducing the iMac—without a floppy disk! Branson, with no experience in it, starting an international airline. Disney, at the depth of the Great Depression, proposing a full-length feature cartoon. "You have to have confidence in nonsense," says airplane designer Burt Rutan, whose aircraft have circled the globe on a single tank of gas, and have climbed to the edge of space as well.[46]

"We build toys," said Nassim Taleb. "Some of those toys change the world."[47]

And now comes the hardest part of the visionary's quest: selling those silly ideas to a skeptical world.

CHAPTER FIVE

Courage and Conviction

By the time Walt Disney was appearing regularly on television in front of millions of kids, his persona—so carefully cultivated by the man himself—was that of Uncle Walt, the relaxed, genial teller of children's tales.

Less well known is the image of Walt as the driven visionary, exceeding his credit, gambling the studio's existence on the next picture, driving away his employees and even his friends, and at times alienating his own family. Walt could be kind and gentle, but when it came to his dream, he could be ruthless. "Unless you were 100 percent for Walt," said one employee, "unless you were doing for him, working for him—he thought you were double-crossing him."[1]

Late at night, when almost everyone else at the studio was home asleep, Walt would be roaming the floor. "There was not a night that we didn't end up in the studio," his wife, Lillian, recalled.[2] By 1931, the pressures were so great—Walt's battles with the film distributors, his arguments with the banks, his growing distance from his own employees—that several of his most loyal friends, including Mickey Mouse creator Ub Iwerks, left Walt to start their own competing studio.

Gaunt and tense, Disney wasn't able to sleep at night. He found himself unable to speak on the phone without bursting into tears.[3] Viewing his latest cartoons and seeing only the flaws, he became physically ill. "I was expecting more from my artists than they were giving me," he said later, "and all I did all day long was pound, pound, pound."[4] Walt's brother, Roy, who ran the business end of the studio, was alarmed. So were Walt's wife and his doctor. Together they tore him from the studio—talking him into a long, meandering vacation. "Walt Disney, the new king of animation and the father of Mickey Mouse," writes Disney biographer Neal Gabler, "had suffered a breakdown."[5]

In visionaries, the drive to see their dreams fulfilled exceeds rational behavior. They are willing to risk their lives and the well-being of themselves and the people around them. It seems to come with the territory—in fact, it defines what a visionary is.

I remember seeing a video of a helicopter landing on a power transmission line packing 500,000 volts. At the controls was Scott Yenzer. Yenzer's company, Haverfield Corporation, repaired high-voltage transmission lines. Before any repair, the power company would turn off the flow of current. But Yenzer started wondering why. He saw birds land on high-voltage transmission lines, preen themselves, and fly away unharmed. If a bird could do it, why couldn't he? If he landed the skids of his helicopter on the line, what would happen? Conventional wisdom said that half a million volts of electricity would ignite the fuel tanks, turning the chopper into a blazing inferno. But would it?[6]

Yenzer kept thinking it over. He talked with helicopter experts, military experts, electrical engineers. He read everything he could find. Nothing said it wasn't possible—but everyone just shook their heads and said don't even try.

But Yenzer did it. How in the world, I asked him, did you reach that decision? It was simple, he replied. One Sunday morning he got up, the weather was good, his wife was asleep. Without waking her, he simply drove out to the airport and climbed into the helicopter. He took it out to a high-voltage transmission line nearby. This would be the day, he decided, and this would be the moment. It was as simple a decision as that.

He brought the metal skids of the chopper within a few feet of the line. He could feel the tremendous vibration of the current running through the line. He was six inches away when a thin arc of electricity leapt from the line to the chopper, wound its way into his helmet microphone—and then leapt into his chin. Another arc of current chewed at his leg. Yenzer fought off the pain long enough to move the chopper closer to the transmission line. Finally, he put the skids down on the line, and held them there. Nothing happened. The fuel tanks didn't explode. The electric current didn't fry the engine or disable its electrical system, as everyone had said it would. He was right, and conventional wisdom was wrong. In that moment he had changed the way that power lines would be repaired from that day forward.

Stanley Williams had a vision as well, but he wasn't as lucky. Williams, a professor at Arizona State University, is a volcano expert. There are plenty of volcano experts that sit safely away from the smoking tops of mountains, studying the data from afar—and then there are a handful of them who don't think they'll get it right unless they are literally hovering over the rim. Williams is one of those.

In 1993 he went to the top of 14,000-foot Volcan Galeras in Colombia. Eight years earlier 23,000 people had died in a matter of hours when another Colombian volcano, Nevado del Ruiz, had blown its top. Now Williams was leading an international team of scientists to the top of Galeras to settle some questions about why volcanoes blow. He says he didn't realize what was about to happen; others have argued that he saw the warning signs but refused to back down. In any case, while he and the other scientists were at the top, Galeras blew.

A rock the size of a baseball smashed into Williams's skull, shoving bone fragments into his brain. A blast of stone followed, shattering his legs, and a flaming glob of magma set his backpack and clothes on fire. Others on the rim were crushed by rocks and killed; five of them who had been in the crater itself were never seen again. Williams spent months in the hospital, and when he recovered enough to walk, he went back up on the volcanoes again.[7]

Most visionaries have no intention of losing their lives for their dreams. But it needn't be death that they are defying. It can be smaller things they risk—like their businesses, their money, and their dreams. This was certainly the case with Andrew Grove, former chairman and CEO of Intel. I met Grove about ten years ago in Santa Clara, California, at an empty shell of a building that had served as Intel's first office and manufacturing plant—17,000 square feet, wires dangling down from the high ceilings, a cold slab of cracked concrete beneath our feet. It wasn't much prettier back in 1968 when Intel moved in. The water pipes leaked, and dust kept seeping in and contaminating the semiconductor chips: It was a former Union Carbide plant that they had hastily made into a semiconductor production facility. As we walked slowly through one corner of the plant, Grove spoke of working long hours to get the 1103 memory chip, Intel's first high-volume semiconductor, into production. But it wasn't easy designing and producing the chip while assuring quality control. "It strained the technology, it strained the design, and it strained our testing abilities," Grove explained. "The code name was 1103. Today I still get a twinge when I look down at my digital watch and it says 11:03."

But Grove was accustomed to adversity. He knew how to fight his way upstream. Born in Hungary in 1936, he survived the Nazi occupation only to grow up scrapping for existence under the Soviet occupation. He got to the United States on a rusty former troop carrier, made his way to Brooklyn, and waited tables while completing a degree in chemical engineering at City College. Moving on to Berkeley, he received his doctorate in chemical engineering in 1963. He was hired by Fairchild Semiconductor shortly thereafter, and five years after that—when he heard that two of Fairchild's stars, Gordon Moore and Bob Noyce, were leaving to start Intel— he insisted on joining them.

Grove had been through a lot, but nothing topped the pressure at Intel: pressure to design a workable commercial chip. Pressure to raise money. Pressure to thwart competitors. And easily the greatest pressure of all—the task of *manufacturing* the semiconductors, which demanded a pristine environment, in the old Union Carbide building. To top that off, Intel had divided its small staff of engineers into competing R&D teams, which raised tensions at the plant to the boiling point. As director of operations, Grove felt every ounce of that pressure. Screaming and arguing were not uncommon. Grove admits that he was as much to blame as anyone. "There was a lot of infighting here," he confessed. "One of the people who reported to me had a nervous breakdown, right in front of my eyes."

For a short period of time in the 1970s, Intel had 100 percent of the memory chip business. Then other competitors rushed in. Most of them failed. But the big bomb hit in the mid-1980s, when the Japanese developed better-quality memory chips than Intel, and flooded the market with them. By 1985, "we had lost our bearings.

We were wandering in the valley of death," Grove recalled in his book *Only the Paranoid Survive*. "I looked out the window at the Ferris wheel of the Great America amusement park revolving in the distance, then I turned back to Gordon [Moore] and I asked, 'If we got kicked out and the board brought in a new CEO, what would he do?' Gordon answered without hesitation, 'He would get us out of memory chips.' I stared at him, numb, then said, 'Why don't you and I walk out the door, come back, and do it ourselves.' "

That's what Intel did. The company shifted its focus almost entirely to microprocessors. And with that, Intel took off again. In 1997, *Time* magazine put Andy Grove on its cover, naming him "Man of the Year."

Two years later we were walking through the old plant. "What went on here is something I cherish," Grove remarked, taking one last look around. "But the lesson I learned was never get involved in another start-up. One was enough for me."

I nodded. "So when did Intel stop feeling like a start-up?" I asked

Grove stopped and thought for a moment. "It hasn't yet," he replied.[8]

Although it may not seem so at first, another "fighter" is the designer Diane von Furstenberg. Von Furstenberg (née Halfin) married a German prince when she was twenty-two and fell easily in with the jet-set crowd in Europe and New York. Home was an Upper East Side apartment and an estate in Milford, Connecticut. Life was a choice between parties in the Hamptons or Paris, or skiing at St. Moritz. Von Furstenberg could have ridden this luxury liner forever. But she was not content with luxury alone. She wanted to make something of herself and, as she explained to me one afternoon, to create something that had never existed before. In 1970, she saw her chance. The clothing at the time was stuck somewhere between unisex pantsuits and '60s hippie; nothing stylish and simple, at least to her taste, was being made. Apprenticing herself to an Italian fabric designer, von Furstenberg created her own line of printed cotton knit dresses, and then brought them to New York. She was seven months pregnant, she recalled, pulling a heavy suitcase full of samples up flights of stairs, taking one rejection after another from the buyers. Her friends thought she had lost her mind. That spring, during New York's famed Fashion Week, she hired some young women from a modeling school to present her work at the Gotham Hotel. A few small shops bought her designs, then Bloomingdale's, then a store on Rodeo Drive in Beverly Hills. She hit the road, lugging her suitcase full of samples from one mom-and-pop clothing store to another. (One time in Flint, Michigan, she recalled, the owner of one store insisted on driving her back to her hotel for the night. She demurred, but he insisted—and then "almost had a heart attack" when they drove up to the Grosse Pointe manor of Henry Ford II and his wife Christina, with Diane sheepishly admitting that *that* was where she was bedding down for the night.)[9]

By the end of 1975, von Furstenberg was selling 15,000 of her figure-hugging "wrap dresses" a week. Retail sales from her clothes, branding licenses, and a new fragrance and cosmetics line hit $60 million. A few months later she was on the front page of the *Wall Street Journal*—and then, the cover of *Newsweek*. "Von Furstenberg: The Princess Who Is Everywhere," the *New York Times* proclaimed. And she was still just twenty-eight years old.

But in 1977, the bubble burst: The company was overextended, the market saturated with her products. *Women's Wear Daily* declared the wrap-dress craze history. Von Furstenberg was stuck with $4 million in inventory—and a factory in Italy pumping out 25,000 new dresses a week. The company was sliding quickly toward bankruptcy.

But von Furstenberg fought back. She sold the entire dress business, despite the emotional toll, and restructured the company top to bottom. She refocused exclusively on cosmetics and perfumes while continuing to make millions a year by licensing her famous DVF brand name. The company took off again—only to overheat and overexpand once more in the early 1980s. The company was nearly lost, until the cosmetic business was sold. Now, with a cash-positive position, von Furstenberg set out to build DVF all over again.

In 1992, she made her most unexpected leap: She brought her DVF signature goods to QVC, the dowdy home shopping network. One night, she recalls, she sold more than $750,000 worth of her goods in just fifteen minutes. When Barry Diller bought QVC, von Furstenberg got 10 percent of the company as a kind of finder's fee.

Since then she has continued to fight for the survival of her firm. Recently she filed lawsuits against several big retailers accusing them of copying her trademarked designs. She's been even tougher on brand counterfeiters, lobbying for congressional passage of what is called the Design Piracy Prohibition Act. Now, some 40 years after setting off a fashion revolution with her wrap dress, von Furstenberg is president of the Council of Fashion Designers of America, the highest seat at the most prestigious fashion association in the nation.

"Isn't it hard," I asked her one day, "fighting one battle after another, to keep your dream alive?"

"My mother was in the concentration camps," Diane replied quietly, "at Auschwitz-Birkenau and Ravensbruck. When she was freed she weighed forty-nine pounds. Sixteen months later she gave birth to me. Compared to that, my hardships are nothing."

Courage and commitment separate the visionary from the dreamer. But what pushes a visionary to risk so much for his or her dream?

There are many ways to answer this question, but let's continue with our exploration of the brain.

As we have seen, the brain is always processing information. Computers are always processing information as well. But the fundamental difference between a computer and a brain is that the brain has *goals*. Not computers: They just don't *care*. For instance, each of Google's computing centers consumes as much power as the entire city of Las Vegas (on a lizard-scorching summer's night). Multiple cooling towers are required to keep the centers from melting down to goo. They can calculate the square root of the universe and answer tens of thousands of questions instantly. But do they really give a hoot? Not at all.

Humans *care*. They have goals, and in the case of visionaries, they will risk their lives, infuriate their business partners, ignore their kids, and abandon their spouses for them. So what pushes humans forward?

Neuroscientists see dopamine, a neurotransmitter, as the agent behind goal setting. Dopamine is derived from neurons that cluster in the brain stem, 25,000 of them on each side of the stem. In the 1960s, scientists placed tiny wires into the dopamine neurons of monkeys and taught them that every time a light went on they would receive a drop of juice. When the monkeys tasted the juice, dopamine flooded their brains. Good stuff! But what the scientists noticed was that very soon the brains of the monkeys rewarded them with dopamine the moment the light went on. They had transferred their source of pleasure from the immediate to the remote. Now you can imagine a visionary working away into the night in the garage, cold, tired—yet with dopamine flowing steadily in the anticipation of the reward to come.[10]

In *The Science of Happiness*, Dr. Stefan Klein writes, "Dopamine is the substance that drives us on. It makes a goal tempting. When dopamine is released, we feel a surge of happiness. It is involved when we attack a new problem." Dopamine seems to encourage us to find patterns, notes Klein. "The feeling that dopamine stimulates enables us to see connections that are otherwise hidden and to combine things that have never been brought together."

Heightened perception is actually a mood lifter, Klein says, because your brain experiences the state of elevated alertness as joyous: "When people visualize what they intend to accomplish, an accompanying bodily response makes them feel the reality of their goal."[11]

It may be simplistic to think of visionaries as dopamine addicts. But that word—addicted—is sometimes used by visionaries themselves in describing their drive. Dopamine makes them tireless, impervious to pain, unable to stop. It convinces them to put up more sail than they should.

It was certainly true in the case of Disney. Coming back to the studio after his breakdown, Disney was healthier but no less ambitious. In story conferences, when he saw something he liked, "he would leap to his feet and be off in a creative convulsion," writes Neal Gabler, "spinning new ideas, one after another, sometimes even shooting down his own contribution and adducing another and then another and another."[12]

Disney had already won a special Oscar for creating the character of Mickey Mouse, and could have retired and played polo for the rest of his life. But by 1936 he was pitting himself against the conventional wisdom: that no one, and certainly no adult, would sit through a full-length feature cartoon. *Snow White*'s budget of $250,000 was soon surpassed, and Disney spent much of his time begging Bank of America for more.

Fortunately for Walt, *Snow White and the Seven Dwarfs* was a hit. The studio raked in millions. Walt received honorary degrees from Harvard and Yale. The studio won a shelf load of Oscars. But there's something you need to know about dopamine: In response to any repeated stimulus, dopamine gradually tapers off. That means a dopamine addict has to seek out a new source (a male lab rat will copulate frantically with a female for a while and then lose interest, until a fresh new female comes by, at which time he will go into high gear again). It is little wonder, then, that serial entrepreneurs are always out there, seeking out one new hit after another.

That was certainly the case with Disney. First he decided to build a magnificent Disney animation studio in nearby Burbank. And he would have a new animated feature as well: *Pinocchio.* It would not only be creatively superior to *Snow White,* Walt boasted, it would be produced faster than *Snow White.* Meanwhile, *Bambi* would be animated simultaneously. Topping that, Disney met Polish-born symphony conductor Leopold Stokowski and together they began to plot an even grander departure from conventional animation—in the form of *Fantasia.*

Walt, whose dark moods had dispelled with the favorable response to *Snow White,* grew ever more intense. He became increasingly tough and ruthless, mercurial and rude. "He could chew you out," recalled one employee. "He could do that real well. He could make you feel mighty darn small."[13] When some of his employees complained about his aloofness, Walt replied tartly, "The men who have worked closely with me to organize and keep the studio rolling . . . should not be envied. Frankly those fellows catch plenty of hell, and a lot of you can feel lucky that you don't have much contact with me."[14] So much for "Uncle" Walt.

Visionaries may be racing toward perceived pleasure, but the case could be made that they're running away as well—running away from pain. In fact, in the choice between pain and pleasure, pain aversion may be the greater force driving a visionary forward.

In *The Wisdom Paradox,* neuropsychologist Elkhonon Goldberg writes, "It has been said that had Prozac been available in the days of the great mariners, they would have popped a pill or two and stayed happily partying in Seville, Lisbon, or Cadiz instead of embarking on their momentous explorations. Perfectly content people do not discover new lands, do not circumvent the globe, and do not create revolutions in science. If everything is hunky-dory, why bother?"[15]

Antonio Damasio seconds that opinion, noting that individuals born with a bizarre condition known as congenital absence of pain do not acquire normal behavioral strategies. "Many seem to be eternally giggly and pleased . . ."[16]

But what is the source of this pain? Many think it is etched into our psyches in infancy and childhood. Says Goleman, in *Emotional Intelligence,* "The interactions of life's earliest years lay down a set of emotional lessons based on the attunement and upsets in the contacts between infant and caretakers."[17] According to neurologist Joseph LeDoux, these are stored in the amygdala as rough blueprints for emotional life.

All of this conjures up the great final scene from *Citizen Kane*— where we see the boy's sled tossed into the furnace, and the flames flickering around the word "Rosebud." It is then that we realize that the entire arc of ruthless ambition that defined Charles Foster Kane's life was an attempt to compensate for uncaring parents and a childhood gone awry.

One can usually lay some blame on the folks: As a teenager, Walt Disney endured his father's temper. Once, Walt even held back his father's arm to keep from being struck with a hammer.[18] When Walt completed his new studio in Burbank—a modernistic, glassy enclave of which he was very proud—his father asked Walt flatly if the building could be used for anything more useful than a cartoon studio. Walt, stumbling over his words, replied that it could be probably converted into a hospital, if the studio failed.[19]

The Wright brothers were brought up by an autocratic, self-centered father as well. When his sons flew at Kitty Hawk, Reverend Wright made a brief note of it in his diary, and then returned to musing over his own activities. But blaming the folks goes only so far. Branson adores his parents, whom he called his best friends. Steve Jobs had loving parents who cleared a space for him on his father's workbench in the garage. So how do you account for these visionaries' gnawing dissatisfaction?

A previous failure may be part of the answer. For instance, Carlo Rubbia tried desperately to convince the Fermi National Accelerator Lab near Chicago to build an experiment to his specs that, he was convinced, would reveal the elusive W and Z particles. After more than a year of pleading, he was rejected, and according to one report, he was even told that his efforts would make him nothing more than a "footnote in history." Stung and bitter, he took his ideas over to CERN, where revenge became the goad and the Nobel the salving balm.[20]

Richard Branson's career was also about rebellion: proving that the little guys could beat the establishment, whether it was record company EMI, which dominated the British music industry, or British Airways, with which Virgin had had an ugly and protracted struggle. As a kid, Branson had a tough time with his academics. When he was eight years old he was sent to a private school in the country. "If you couldn't spell or couldn't add up or couldn't remember that the area of a circle is 'pi r squared,'" he recalled in his autobiography, "then the solution was simple: you were beaten until you did." He later realized that he had dyslexia, but it didn't matter. "When I gave the inevitable wrong answer, it was either more lines or a beating. I almost grew to prefer the beatings since at least they were quick." Later, when he attended private school at Stowe, his grades were not much better. He also got the reputation of being a bit of a rebel. He kept badgering the faculty, for instance, for changes in tradition—like scrapping the Saturday sports program and shaking up the seating in the dining hall. Eventually he started a newspaper in which he could vent his opinions and publish those of others. When Branson finally graduated, his headmaster's parting words were ambivalent at best: "Congratulations, Branson. I predict that you will either go to prison or become a millionaire."[21]

Even Walt Disney had something to prove. When his little animation studio in Kansas City failed, Walt declared bankruptcy, and at his brother's urging decided to move to California. While on the train west, Walt struck up a conversation with a fellow passenger. The man noted that he was in the entertainment business in L.A. The young Walt eagerly offered that he was too. At that, the man asked what line of work Walt was in. When Disney said, "Cartoonist," the man gave him such a look of condescension that Walt never forgot it.[22] No wonder he worked tirelessly to make animation into an art.

At the age of twenty-two Diane von Furstenberg found herself unmarried, pregnant, and about to marry into a German family that looked down on her. "I remember taking a walk in [the] garden alone," she reflected, "talking to the child I was carrying, and saying out loud that I was going to be successful to prove myself to this disapproving family. I had this fire in me both for me and for the baby inside me. Together we would show the world."[23]

In *iCon: Steve Jobs—The Greatest Second Act in the History of Business,* coauthors Jeffrey S. Young and William L. Simon describe Steve Jobs as the kid in school who was always the loner. He wasn't a jock, or an academic overachiever, or even a nerd that other nerds felt comfortable around, they noted. While Jobs displayed a sharp wit, he rarely laughed. He was intense: He stared at people. When he did speak, he often drew so close that he invaded the other person's space. At best, he was a "wirehead," a geek absorbed in electronics. In fact, it was no doubt a relief for Jobs, after the social pressures of school, to go home to the garage—where his father had built him a workbench—and lose himself in tinkering. Jobs grew more antiestablishment as the flower-power revolution bloomed in nearby San Francisco. By the time he was sixteen he was wearing threadbare jeans and walking around barefoot with his hair down to his shoulders. Left to make his own choices, he began to skip school.

But accompanying this was Jobs's search for meaning. Eventually, this search led him to India.

As soon as he and friend (and eventual Apple employee) Dan Kottke arrived in Delhi, Jobs tossed his ragged jeans and donned a lungi, the sarong often worn by beggars. They slept by the side of the road, begged food, and for several months journeyed up the foothills into the Himalayas, seeking enlightenment from various mystical yogis and babas, or holy men. "At some deep level there was an insecurity that Steve had to go out and prove himself," Kottke told Young and Simon in an interview.

Whatever the drive, Kottke and Jobs ended up in rural India, covered with fleas and lice (and hence with their heads shaved), sunburned and emaciated, wearing sandals and cotton shawls. They were sleeping in a dry creek bed one night when a horrific thunderstorm rolled in over them. "There we were," Kottke recalled, "wearing next to nothing, and I remember us hunkering down in the sand trying to defend ourselves from the rain pelting down, trying to dig a hole that we could crawl into so that the rain wouldn't destroy us."[24]

Jobs returned from India enlightened, but not in the way he had expected. "It was one of the first times that I started realizing that maybe Thomas Edison did a lot more to improve the world than

Karl Marx and Neem Karoli Baba put together," he told *Rolling Stone*. That was the epiphany that guided his life from then on: After returning, Jobs still wandered around threadbare and barefoot, still practiced Zen Buddhism. But now he saw the computer boards that he and Steve Wozniak were making as a mission, not merely a business. Personal computers would save the world. They'd put power into the hands of the people. And Apple was in the vanguard of the revolution.

When Jobs asked John Sculley to leave Pepsi and join him at Apple in the winter of 1983, it was with the now-famous words "Do you want to spend the rest of your life selling sugared water, or do you want a chance to change the world?"[25] A few months later, when Sculley did join Apple, Jobs was ecstatic. "There's something going on here," he said. "There's something that's changing the world, and this is the epicenter."[26]

Beyond the need to prove oneself, to wreak revenge, even to develop an idea that will shake the earth and liberate the masses, is there some other goad—something even more fundamental—that forces visionaries forward?

Burt Rutan was waiting for me just outside the office of his airplane-designing plant on the edge of the Mojave Desert in California. His blue eyes squinted against the hot sun, and with his muttonchop sideburns he looked more like a hot rod mechanic than an aeronautics genius. But Rutan had designed one impossibly brilliant airplane after the next—airplanes that looked like they were flying backward, built of the kind of composite materials you'd see in surfboards and ski boats rather than airplanes—each one an evolutionary step forward in performance.[27]

Rutan began in 1967 with the Model 27 VariViggen, a 19-foot airplane built in his garage and wind-tested atop his Dodge Dart as it sped at top speed across the Mojave at night. Following that first airplane, one new model followed another in quick succession. By the mid-1980s radically new designs were flying out of the Rutan workshop at the rate of two or three a year.

I watched Rutan lay his hand on one of his latest creations. It was called the Boomerang—an airplane that to most eyes seemed all out of kilter, as though it had been made of hot plastic and pulled at the corners. The left wing was slightly ahead of the right wing; the engines were set off balance. Why? Rutan told me that the opposing rotation of propellers makes planes fly slightly sideways anyhow, so why not put them off balance in the first place? Besides, traditional two-engine planes are difficult to fly if one engine goes out. But this plane, with its asymmetrical design, would fly on one engine almost as well as on two. So why not built it asymmetrical to begin with? I looked at it suspiciously.

"Want to go for a ride?" he asked with a sly grin.

Looking at the list of Rutan's airplanes makes you think that maybe something else is going on that drives visionaries to do what they do.

In the mid-1700s the French philosopher Nicolas de Condorcet introduced the idea of "progress" as the steady climb by mankind toward a better world. Thomas Jefferson and Benjamin Franklin were advocates. For them, progress was seen as a particularly American thing. Manifest Destiny, meanwhile—in which Americans supposedly had a divine right to expand from the Atlantic to the Pacific—also implied that the steam engines, railroad lines, telegraphs, and other technologies needed to get us there were also somehow part of a divine plan.

Benjamin Franklin said that "man is a tool-making animal." In *Scenario Visualization,* the philosopher Robert Arp notes that while several animals make tools, only humans make tools that *make* tools. We do this through our powers of visualization, he says, which enables us to imagine things that have never existed before. "We can invent new tools based on mental blueprints," he says, "synthesizing concepts which, at first glance, seem wholly disparate or unrelated, and devise novel solutions to problems."[28]

Visionaries are not interested in the past. They are fixed on the next big thing. Indeed, when I met with Rutan, he agreed to talk with me about his airplanes *only* if I would listen to him describe his next big thing: a spaceship. I indulged him and he went on and on about a Flash Gordon–esque contraption with a bulbous nose and porthole windows all around. At $150,000 a ticket, Rutan said, he could turn space flight into the world's greatest roller coaster. So much for the sanctity and nobility of space travel, I recall reflecting. Rutan had the restless urge of a visionary—welded tightly to the instincts of a carnival worker.

Watching visionaries fight their way forward, like salmon thrashing their way upstream, you can't help but wonder if they are agents in something even more fundamental.

Some thinkers have suggested that the tools we make are part of biological evolution, not separate from it. That human beings, unlike most living things, evolve not only through their organic beings, but through the things they create. A hammer is an evolutionary improvement, since it is an extension of an arm, just as a telescope is an extension of the vision provided by the eye. A computer, in its limited way, is an extension of the brain. Recently, for instance, scientists have shown that the brain actually reads the extension of the arm that a hammer provides and adjusts its map of the body accordingly—otherwise, we could never hit a nail. "To be accurate in doing an action with a tool, you need to make the tool become a part of your body," Lucilla Cardinali of the French National Institute for Health and Medical Research told *The Scientist* magazine.[29]

In 1957, biologist Julian Huxley also noted the cumulative impact of tools and ideas. "Man's inherited mental powers cannot have changed appreciably since the time of the Aurignacian cave-dwellers," he wrote in *Knowledge, Morality and Destiny.* "What has changed is the ease in which those powers are used, and the social and ideological frameworks which condition their use."[30]

He continues, "Once the cumulative transmission of experience was available, and accordingly, mind as well as matter became capable of self-reproduction and self-variation, it was inevitable that evolution would take place overwhelmingly in the cultural rather than in the biological sphere, and with an enormous acceleration of tempo . . ."

Huxley's words foreshadowed those of evolutionary biologist Richard Dawkins. In his 1976 blockbuster *The Selfish Gene,* Dawkins shook up the field of evolutionary science, suggesting that evolution was not about different species bettering themselves, but about the genes in every living thing trying to get the greatest advantage possible. (It is not a certain species of bird that is pushing its way forward, then, but the genes in each living thing trying to outdo all the other genes.)

Dawkins posited another idea. He said that "cultural artifacts"—such as ideas, fashions, and rituals—were methods of evolution. Dawkins dubbed these agents memes. Memes are the way that humans store and communicate collective wisdom, rather than reinventing the world with every new generation, he explained. In a subsequent book, *The Extended Phenotype,* Dawkins added tools and technology to the evolutionary arsenal.

With memes and extended phenotypes, the survival of the fittest is played out not merely with genetic competition but with things—which tribe had the stronger bow, which kingdom had the stronger catapult, which nation had the better navy, and which nation adopted the best form of capitalism or employed the best scientific method. Or even which nation built a better luxury car, thereby winning the most favorable balance of trade. Evolution, in other words, had leapt from behind the glacially slow genesis of biology into the fast lane of human technology and innovation.

Could this be the primal force driving the courage, conviction, hardheadedness, and callousness of visionaries? Are they seized not only by the dopamine pumping through their brains, by the echoes of unresolved conflicts, by the dissonance between what should be and what is, but also, and more profoundly, by some evolutionary drive to be fitter than what existed before? For anyone striving to understand why visionaries would thrash themselves upstream, risking death, this is not an inconceivable idea at all.

Huxley described improvements in technology as a kind of "cultural evolution." He said, "These resemble in an interesting way the trends of improvement to be seen in biological evolution: both types of trends continue in the same general direction for a considerable period of time, until they reach a limit of some sort, when they become stabilized (and often enfeebled, reduced, or extinguished)."[31]

If one were to demand evidence that an evolutionary process is involved in making things, one only has to visit a museum of technology to see the fruits of this process. At the Museum of Science and Technology in Chicago, you can see a lineup of steam engines, starting with wagons with water tanks and firing boxes crudely bolted on, to the apex of steam locomotion—a grand, fire-breathing steam locomotive that could top out at 100 miles per hour.

At the San Diego Air and Space Museum you can see a progression in airplane technology that starts with cloth and wooden spars and ends in jet engines and modern composite material designs.[32]

There *are* marked similarities between biological and technological evolution. This became evident to Niles Eldredge, curator in the

Department of Invertebrates at the American Museum of Natural History in New York. At the museum, Eldredge has assembled 1,000 individual specimens of mollusks, rotifers, spiders, and fish by genealogical group, a display that stretches for some 90 feet through the Hall of Biodiversity. But at home he is an avid collector of nineteenth-century cornets, the brass musical instrument. He has carefully arranged his collection of 500 "species" of cornets in taxonomic relationships of shape, style, and date of manufacture. What is striking is the similarity in the evolution of living things and of man-made things—even in terms of the evolution of a cornet.[33]

You can push the similarity between technological and biological evolution only so far, of course. Designers can borrow from each other—such as when one cornet maker sees the improvement made by a competitor and adopts it. In biology, that doesn't happen. Also, when living things die out, they cannot reappear. Technology can disappear for a while, and then reemerge.

But in terms of what *drives* visionaries, you cannot ignore that they are always trying to make something that (in their eyes, at least) is *better*. Walt Disney began with flickering stick figures in his Laugh-O-Gram *Adventures of Alice* and progressed to the level of *Snow White* and beyond. (What many people miss in the progression of Disney films are the technological achievements— from the tighter synchronization of sound to animated cartoons to the invention of the multiplane camera that brought a three-dimensional quality to the Disney classics.) Jobs began with the first Apple-1 machine and evolved to the iPad. Rubbia discovered the W and Z particles, and then immediately lobbied for money to build a newer, bigger, more expensive machine to hunt for the elusive materials called quarks. Each of these visionaries drove themselves (and those around them) nearly mad in their quest for something better.

The paleontologist Jack Sepkoski noted that 98 percent of the species that ever lived on earth are now extinct. We don't even know what we have missed. And, indeed, you can see it happening in the physical things of life as well: buggy whips, bustles, vacuum tubes, brown bottles that once contained snake oil. The Smithsonian Institution and countless other museums are full of them. If technology is an evolutionary race, as Huxley and Dawkins suggest, you can't help wondering what technology in, say, a million years, will have survived. And what will be the 98 percent that is gone?

Amazon.com founder Jeff Bezos—a visionary himself—touched on this recently when he discussed the relationship of printed books to Amazon's digital book reader, the Kindle. "The book really has had a 500-year run. It's probably the most successful technology ever," he said. "If Gutenberg were alive today, he would recognize the physical book and know how to operate it immediately. Given how much change there has been everywhere else, what's remarkable is how stable the book has been for so long. But no technology, not even one as elegant as the book, lasts forever."[34] And someday, I suppose, we won't remember that it existed at all.

By 1939, the Disney business was suffering from Walt's unflagging enthusiasm. The new studio in Burbank had cost nearly $3 million. While fiscal 1939 saw a profit of $1.25 million, 1940 was on its way to a loss of $1.25 million. Roy Disney had traveled several times to New York to investigate with investment bankers the idea of issuing long-term debentures or even public stock.

My father, who had joined Disney as an animator when he was still in his teens (the age of the average employee then was about twenty), was a friend of both Walt and Roy. (My mother also worked at the Disney studio; in fact, my parents met at the studio commissary.)

Because of that bond, the Disney brothers were not an abstraction; they were a living presence in our home.

By 1940 my father had been drafted into the U.S. Army and was stationed in New York City. Roy Disney, in town on business, took my father out to dinner, as he often did. The following day, my father wrote a troubled letter to my mother in California. *Pinocchio,* he told her, was an economic drain on the company. Roy was worried sick. In his letter, my father said he didn't know if the studio would survive it.

Indeed, *Pinocchio,* when it premiered on February 7, 1940, was a financial bomb. America's audiences, already watching the war spread through Europe, were not filling the theater seats to see this dark tale. Nor were the reviews nearly as good as those that *Snow White* had received.

But Disney's success didn't stop with *Pinocchio.* Disney pushed the studio on to *Fantasia, Dumbo, Bambi, Cinderella, Alice in Wonderland, Peter Pan,* and more. Then came the live-action films and television, and finally the most unexpected feat of all, the vision bridging films with Disneyland and Walt Disney World.

Whenever Disney achieved a goal, he moved the game forward. It never stopped. When, in 1966, he was diagnosed with lung cancer, he was still reading scripts late into the night, still debating with the animators of *The Jungle Book* whether a tiger could really climb a tree, and still planning Disney World—and traveling the country trying to round up corporate sponsors for EPCOT, his "Experimental Prototype Community of Tomorrow."

In the end, lying in his hospital bed with his brother Roy standing at his side, Walt would look at the ceiling tiles overhead and, raising his finger, trace his plans for EPCOT against them. Every four tiles represented a square mile. This is where the highway will go, Walt would say. This is where the monorail will run.[35]

Walt passed away on December 15, 1966, at the age of sixty-five. He died as he had lived, a fighter. If you had reeled back the years to 1941, you would have seen him standing before an assembly of his workers. They were trying to unionize the Disney studios, and Walt, hurt and defensive, was fighting back. "I want to say that I have given twenty years of hard work, I have battled against some very heavy odds. I have sacrificed and I have gambled to bring this business to the place where it is now," he said. His eyes swept their young faces. "Don't forget this—it's the law of the universe that the strong shall survive and the weak must fall by the way—and I don't give a damn what idealistic plan is cooked up; nothing can change that."[36]

CHAPTER SIX

Scaling up the Vision

"I'm going up in my airplane tomorrow and I wondered if you'd like to come along?" Branson asked me over the phone one morning.

I didn't know that Branson even *owned* a plane, but I immediately imagined a Sopwith Camel and Branson standing beside it, sporting a leather helmet, goggles, and a silk scarf. I agreed, and made plans to meet him the next morning at London's Gatwick Airport.

You can imagine my surprise the next day when I found out that the airplane was not a biplane, but a double-decker Boeing 747. As I was seating myself midsection by a window, I spotted Branson's megawatt smile approaching. "Now you're probably wondering where we're off to," he said playfully as he dropped into the seat next to mine. "Well, I can't tell you. You'll just have to wait and see."

We took off, and for a while I gazed out the window at the long wing of the jet. Then, and quite suddenly, we began to cut into a tight circle. The wing fell at a steeper angle beneath us, and

I found myself wondering, a bit nervously, if passenger planes like this were made to endure such acrobatics. We had made only a few circles when I began to see that we were descending onto a little island below, a speck, really, in the North Sea. As we descended farther, I could make out fields, a church spire, several buildings, and what seemed to be a tiny airstrip below us. Another circle or two, and I noticed lots of people—in fact, what looked like the entire population—hurrying toward the airfield. I couldn't see their faces, but I imagined that they were looking up, wondering why this massive aircraft was in a descending spiral over their little island.

We were getting closer when, bang, the pilot lowered the landing gear. I looked out the window again. Now everyone on the island—men, women, children, horses, dogs, and cats—were running as fast as they could *away* from the tiny airstrip. It was obvious that they had never seen a Boeing 747 land on their 100 yards or so of tarmac.

We came screaming down upon the runway. But just as our rear tires touched the asphalt—with a plume of blue smoke—the pilot pulled back on the stick and, with what must have been a tremendous roar of our engines, shot us straight up into the sky. At that I heard yelps and cheers from the front of the plane, led, I have no doubt, by Branson himself.

We finally returned to London and landed. The pilot emerged from the cockpit. We gathered around him, our hearts still racing. I'll never forget his exclamation: "That's the most fun I've had since the Korean War!"[1]

It would be nice to think that Branson had taken a special liking to me. And I hope he did. But beyond that I realized that I was playing an important role in his visionary quest: In the parlance of networking theorists (who study how ideas spread), I was a *node* in his greater scheme of things. In fact, as a front-page writer for the *Wall Street Journal*—a newspaper with a circulation of more than two million readers and perhaps twice that internationally—I was an *influential* node.[2]

In *The Tipping Point,* Malcolm Gladwell uses a different term. He calls people who have a wide number and range of acquaintances "Connectors." Some Connectors not only know a lot of people, but they have something important to convey, and they're pretty good at broadcasting it. Paul Revere (who, Gladwell notes, was "the man with the biggest Rolodex in colonial Boston") is a perfect example. On his midnight ride on April 18, 1775, Revere alerted the patriots to the British march on Lexington. It spread like a contagion, setting church bells ringing and drums pounding and colonists running in their little silver-buckled shoes all over New England.[3]

Similarly, through the pages of the *Wall Street Journal*—and entirely by proxy ("the power of the press," as was once said)—I knew a million-plus readers. So if Branson was lucky, I would be his Paul Revere, riding up the coast (with a different message, of course: The Virgins are coming!) but with similar effect.

The cumulative power of such networks is remarkable. Demonstrating this was a remarkable study by Nicholas A. Christakis of Harvard University and James H. Fowler of the University of California at San Diego. According to their work, every one of us is within not only six degrees of separation from everyone else, but also three degrees of influence. Everything we do ripples through our friends (for a first-degree effect), our friends' friends (the second degree), and finally our friends' friends' friends (third degree). Then the ripple effect subsides.

Christakis and Fowler calculated that if you have 20 social contacts, and each of these has a similar number of social contacts, you are indirectly connected to 400 people at two degrees of separation, and at one more step (the third degree, or $20 \times 20 \times 20$), some 8,000 people. Now if you consider that the *Wall Street Journal* has millions of readers, the potential impact is enormous.[4]

Some contacts are better than others. A number of research firms customize and sell mailing/e-mail/Twitter lists of "influentials" for their clients. A Boston-based research firm called Traackr, for instance, collects lists of influencers based on their "reach" (how big their audience is, based on the traffic on their personal and social network sites), their "resonance" (how far stories travel when the influencer talks about them), and their "relevance" (how relevant they are to the issue at hand).[5]

So my employment at the *Journal* would be a big winner in terms of reach. And even more so since the Branson story would eventually appear not only on the front page of the paper but on the right-hand column (called Column 6). This was the most prestigious corner of a very prestigious publication. In terms of resonance, typical *Wall Street Journal* readers have a wide circle of friends, associates, and other contacts. And in terms of relevance, the typical *Wall Street Journal* reader has a strong interest in the world of business, and especially in entrepreneurs as colorful as Branson himself.

If that weren't enough, I was also what network theorists call a "weak tied" link. Is that a good thing? Absolutely: Branson at the time was already well known to the British press. But I was an outsider, a correspondent from America, a "weak tied link" at a time when the name Richard Branson meant almost nothing in the States. Since I was not a member of the existing Branson network (mostly the UK and Europe), I was a bridge across the Atlantic to a whole new network.[6]

Once spread across America, the story would hopefully have the same effect as Paul Revere's ride. It's the idea that one positive mention leads to another, and another, and another. Eventually the story hits that place Malcolm Gladwell made famous as the "tipping point," at which time the story becomes bigger than the sum of its parts. It now has a life of its own.[7]

What's remarkable is how rapidly and easily we succumb to this cultural influenza. In one experiment, researchers put 15 research assistants together on a sidewalk. When one of the 15 assistants looked up to a sixth-story window, 4 percent of the people passing by did so as well. When all 15 assistants looked up, 40 percent of the other pedestrians did.[8] The fact is that we like to follow the crowd. No wonder we buy songs based on what's popular, or books based on how many effusive reviews they receive. It's no surprise that restaurant owners put their first customers at the front windows, for all to see. Success breeds success.

We even pass our emotional vibes from one to another. In a study of 12,000 interconnected people in Framingham, Massachusetts, for instance, health researchers Christakis and Fowler found that happiness passes from one person to another like the flu. The closer you are to someone happy, the happier you will be. In fact, the two professors even mapped the network: You could actually see the concentrations of happy people and unhappy people, clustering like grapes on the vine. "We found that each happy friend a person has increases that person's probability of being happy by about 9 percent," they noted in *Connected: The Surprising Power of Our Social Networks and How They Shape Our Lives*. "Each unhappy friend decreases it by 7 percent."[9]

The explosive force of contagion, as applied to new ideas and progress, was most memorably described by MIT professor Thomas E. Kuhn in *The Structure of Scientific Revolutions* (a work that the [London] *Times Literary Supplement* called one of "the hundred most influential books since the Second World War"). It was Kuhn, in fact, who coined the term "Paradigm Change." A paradigm change, he said, was both unprecedented enough to pull a group of adherents away from competing modes of scientific activity and still open-ended enough to leave all sorts of problems for others to solve. While Kuhn spoke mostly of scientific paradigms, his thinking certainly applies to technological breakthroughs and the lives of visionary entrepreneurs as well.

In particular, Kuhn noted that the makers of paradigm changes must attract supporters. "At the start," he wrote, "a new candidate for a paradigm may have few supporters, and on occasion the supporter's motives may be suspect. Nevertheless, if they are competent, they will improve it, explain its possibilities, and show what it would be like . . . If the paradigm is destined to win its fight, the number and strength of the persuasive arguments in its favor will increase."[10]

All successful visionaries have learned how to promote their ideas, whether they like it or not. The Wright brothers—with starched collars and stiffer personalities—learned how to schmooze the press in order to defend the patents they had placed on their flying machine. And that image we have today of Henry Ford—aloof, squinty-eyed, and unapproachable—may have been the older Henry Ford, but when he was starting out in 1903 as a maverick car builder, Ford romanced the media. "I will build a motorcar for the multitude," Ford told the press, in a populist sentiment remarkably similar to Jobs's dream for the everyman's personal computer.

"When I launched the airline," Branson writes in his autobiography, "I realized that I would have to use myself to raise the profile of Virgin Atlantic and build the value of the brand. Most companies don't acknowledge the press and have a tiny press office tucked away out of sight." Branson said he makes sure not to do that. "Every day I receive a bundle of press cuttings—everything that mentions Virgin," he added. "These—and staff letters—are the first things I read in the morning."[11]

No, it's not vanity. Branson has said the he's actually quite shy;

stepping into an interview is not something he's ever been comfortable with. Most visionaries, in fact, don't seem to be natural extroverts. Still, they are on a mission; they are pragmatic; and, as we have seen, they are driven. And so they will suffer fools gladly, or at least patiently—even the ink-stained wretches from the world's top publications.

The last time I saw Branson in person was in Orlando, Florida, about ten years after he dive-bombed his 747. Branson was performing a different kind of feat: He was preparing to water-ski behind the Virgin blimp—the first time (I was told) that any person had water-skied behind a dirigible. It would herald Virgin's cross-Atlantic service to Orlando.

As Branson stepped into the muddy rim of this particular lake, I was struck that this person wading in among the lily pads and reeds had dined with the queen, partied with the Rolling Stones, and could be relaxing on his private island (in the *Virgin* Islands, of course). Instead, he was performing for a local TV crew and a few children, with their mothers, who had assembled at the edge of the lake. Standing there, knee-deep in the water, he seemed strangely alone.

The blimp circled around, trailing the ski rope and plastic handle. As it approached us, Branson, now submerged in the lake with the points of his skis protruding, gave us a smile—a grimace, really. "I hope it doesn't break my back," he quipped with a Teddy Roosevelt–esque gnashing of teeth. The handle arced around to his left; he lunged for it, and then off he went, legs splaying out above the skis, his free hand waving at the curiosity seekers gathered along the shore.

Visionaries must convince and coddle the media. But if they want to bring their dreams to life, they must, in the words of Kuhn, "explain its possibilities" to an array of others as well. They especially must create an aura that draws people to come work for them. In the early years of Apple, for instance, the mere rumor that the company was hiring would cause thousands of people to literally surround the building, many of them camping out, sleeping in tents. People don't just coalesce around thin air. The visionary is the magnet.

We've all known people with high intelligence but little in the way of personal magnetism. They don't communicate well, or simply have little to say. They can be negative and uncooperative. People sense it; they feel uncomfortable in their presence. I had lunch once with a private school math teacher who had just been fired. He broke into tears as he explained his predicament. It was heartbreaking. Later I learned that he had two doctoral degrees— one in physics, the other in mathematics—from two of the best universities in the world. He had the smarts, in other words; he just wasn't able to relate to other people.[12]

Now, there undoubtedly have been social misfits who have been great visionaries. In fact, history is full of them. But the kind of visionary I am describing here—that Thomas Kuhn dubbed the *maker* of paradigms—doesn't have the luxury of retreating to an island or an ivory tower. Visionaries know that. And that's why those who succeed are particularly good at drawing people to their causes. But how do they do that? What quality do they have that attracts people to their dreams?

I think it is best stated in two words that I mentioned earlier: emotional intelligence.[13] Emotional intelligence is that rare balance between dry logic and emotional intuition. It manifests itself in a person who can draw from both the analytical and the emotional sides of the human mind. Visionaries, I suspect, have deeper emotional keels than the rest of us. They have to, because the storms they endure are far greater than most of us could handle.

Emotional intelligence seems to draw from the brain's frontal lobe. Patients with frontal lobe injuries can be quite normal and high-functioning, but the greater the extent of the damage, the more emotionally flat and disengaged they are. The side of the frontal lobe also seems to make a difference in emotional orientation. People who display a lot of activity in the left frontal lobe seem to be more cheerful, social, and self-confident. Those with more activity in the right are more apt to be moody—to see the world in darker tones. Supporting that are studies of dozens of babies: Of those who cried when their mothers left the room, all had more brain activity on the right side. Those who did not had more activity on the left.[14]

In addition to the frontal lobe, the amygdala plays a major role. When patients within fMRI machines are asked about the feelings of others, the amygdala lights up with activity. When monkeys had the connection between the amygdala and their cortical pathway severed, notes Goleman, they lived normally except that they could not relate emotionally to the other monkeys as before. Some would withdraw from their colleagues' friendly gestures, and others would run and hide.

Neuroscientist Antonio Damasio sees emotional intelligence rising from neurochemicals as well. Oxytocin, he says, facilitates social interactions. So does serotonin: Monkeys with a high number of serotonin-2 receptors have high social skills, but monkeys with a low number of serotonin-2 receptors do not.[15]

While all human brains are, in general, similar, they are all different in the details. Notes neurologist Joseph LeDoux, "The key to individuality . . . is not to be found in the overall organization of the brain," he says in *The Synaptic Self,* "but in the fine tuning of the underlying neurons." Damasio likens the "degrees of individual topographical variation" among brains to the variations in faces, "which are similar but infinitely diverse . . . because of small anatomical differences in size, contour, and positions of the invariant parts." And so, just as we are born with different brains, some of us are blessed with more emotional intelligence than others. Of course, we all know people who have a natural gift for human interaction, and others who are socially awkward or inept. The good news for the rest of us is that some degree of emotional intelligence can be learned.[16]

Emotional intelligence seems to include a great power to read others. It's interesting to note that a *real* smile emanates from the pleasure center (limbic cortices) of the brain. It then radiates to the muscles that lift the mouth (*zygomaticus major*) and the muscles that lift the cheeks, crinkle the flesh around the eye, and bend the lateral border of the eyebrow (*orbicularis oculi pars lateralis*).

Since the *orbicularis oculi* are not voluntary muscles, notes neuroscientist Michael Gazzaniga, fake smiles can lift the mouth and—with some squeezing—raise the cheeks and squint the eyes. But they can't bend the border of the eyebrow. Knowing that, you can spot the difference between a real smile and a toadying grin.[17]

What's interesting is that most of us are capable of making instinctive, accurate assessments about others. Recall the earlier study of how subjects could read the success of a professor through a six-second video clip? What's surprising is that when the clips were reduced to two seconds each, the outcome was nearly the same.[18]

It seems that we all can read people pretty well. But visionaries either have that skill better honed or merely trust in it more than the rest of us. "I make up my mind about whether I can trust someone within 60 seconds of meeting them," Branson noted in his memoirs.[19]

I remember Branson telling me that he heard a knock on his door one day in the early 1970s, opened it, and saw a scruffy kid standing there, who introduced himself as Simon, his long-lost cousin from South Africa. "I didn't even know I had a long-lost cousin from South Africa," Branson said, laughing. But after eyeing the kid on the front step for a few seconds, Branson invited him in—and told him to stay for the night. Simon Draper (actually a *second* cousin) went on to become Branson's trusted ear on the music scene, and helped build Virgin Records into a billion-dollar business.

Steve Jobs is also known to make quick, and generally prescient, choices about people. He handpicked the people to start Apple, and when he returned in 1997, he spent weeks separating the wheat from the chaff—and having the chaff summarily fired. Disney was also a quick read, and would hire people after a glance at their portfolios and a quick look into their faces.

Visionaries are equally abrupt rejecting those who don't fit in. Jobs has been particularly cruel on occasion. One time, recalls Andy Hertzfeld (who joined Apple in 1981 and became one of the main authors of the Macintosh system software), Jobs eyed a job candidate and immediately knew he was the wrong fit. To the horror of those at the meeting, Jobs began to pound the applicant with crazy questions: How long had he been a virgin? When was the last time he dropped LSD? When the befuddled interviewee tried to reply, as Hertzfeld relates in *Revolution in the Valley,* Jobs retorted, "Gobble, gobble, gobble." It was an example of merciless high-tech hazing.[20]

To be sure, even visionaries can get blindsided. Nearly every visionary story has a Brutus that betrays the leader. As the business expands, spawning jealousy and greed, betrayal is almost inevitable. Steve Jobs was taken in by John Sculley—and learned his lesson when Sculley had him kicked out of the Apple empire. A number of Disney's early employees betrayed him, forming a competing company. These included Ub Iwerks, who had created Mickey Mouse, and who owned 20 percent of the company.

Branson, in the early days of his business, was nearly thrown out in a coup orchestrated by his business partner and childhood friend Nik Powell (they later reconciled and went on with Simon Draper to build Virgin Records together). Disney eventually brought Ub Iwerks back into the fold as well.

Visionaries are particularly good at persuasion, and they certainly know how to charm. One of the most interesting scenes in Gil Amelio's account of his 500 days as CEO of Apple came late in his tenure, when he and his wife met Jobs for dinner. Amelio had met Jobs once before (Jobs had been exiled from the company years earlier by Sculley), but Amelio's wife had never met Jobs—and was apprehensive. But not to worry, Amelio recalled—the dinner went off fabulously, and his wife, not easily impressed, remarked at what a lovely person Jobs was. Three days later, Amelio discovered that he was being fired, and that Jobs, having met with the board, would take his place. He felt, in retrospect, that the dinner was a setup, and that Jobs's warmth had been used to get him to lower his guard and speak more freely than perhaps he should have. "I've never really been taken in by anyone before," Amelio noted in *On the Firing Line: My 500 Days at Apple*. "But I was totally taken in by Steve Jobs, and I really felt like an idiot."[21]

In *Revolution in the Valley,* Andy Hertzfeld described what Apple employees have come to know well: Jobs's "reality distortion field." "It is a confounding mélange of a charismatic rhetorical style, and indomitable will," wrote Hertzfeld, "and an eagerness to bend any fact to fit the purpose at hand. If one line of argument failed to persuade, he would deftly switch to another. Sometimes he would throw you off balance by suddenly adopting your position as his own, without acknowledging that he ever thought differently . . . We would often discuss potential techniques for grounding it, but after a while most of us gave up, accepting it as a force of nature."

Walt Disney had precisely the same "reality distortion field."[22] In Don Peri's *Working With Walt: Interviews with Disney Artists,* animator Campbell Grant noted how Disney would sit slumped during a story meeting, listening without enthusiasm to what he was hearing, drumming his fingers nervously on the arms of his chair (much to the terror of the employee presenting the story line), and then, a week or two later, "he'd come into your room full of enthusiasm, and he'd sell you back your own idea." Animation director Dave Hand had a similar experience: "I've sat in story meetings with Walt and heard someone bring up a spontaneous gag . . . Walt's sitting there, frowning, looking usually someplace else, and before the meeting is over, *he* gets the idea out of the air, excitedly explains it, and it goes in the picture."[23]

Visionaries are driven to express their dreams, whatever the reaction or resistance of the receiver. They are evangelists for the cause, indefatigable in their compulsion to pass the story forward to those around them. When Don Peri interviewed Ben Sharpsteen, one of Disney's earliest and most prolific animators and directors, Sharpsteen recalled this instance of Walt's irrepressible nature:

I had gone to a restaurant to have my evening meal, and as I was leaving, Walt and his wife Lilly were coming in to have their dinner at the same lunch counter . . . I could not get through the door because Walt stood there. He wanted to tell me about a picture that we were going to make . . . Mickey Mouse is going to give a revue of performances by the barnyard animals with himself as the master of ceremonies. There is going to be a balcony, the roof of an outhouse, and all the cats will be up there. Walt described each act and the audience response. As each act follows, the applause gets more enthusiastic, and finally when the big act comes, everybody goes crazy with applause and the cats are whooping it up and jumping so much that they all break through the roof of the outhouse.

The sides fall apart, exposing a hole in the ground where naturally the cats have disappeared and this is where we "iris" right out with "The End." It took a few minutes for Walt to tell this story. We were in a public eating place and I did not know who might be trying to get in or get out, but of course I had to stand there and listen to Walt. I noticed that his wife was standing to one side and that she was not too enthusiastic. When Walt pulled the final punch about the cats all going out of sight, she said, "Humph, I don't think I want to see that picture." Even though her remark was very much to the point, it did not affect Walt the least bit, because we went right ahead and made the picture.[24]

The enthusiasm of visionaries is understandable. But what makes us go along with them? Brain studies have identified "mirror neurons," which apparently link observation to imitation. Mirror neurons play a part in learning—for instance, as we watch a teacher play the guitar. Every movement of another, it seems, is tracked. In one experiment, a group of subjects watched someone move his finger: This was enough to illuminate the same part of the brain (seen via fMRI) as if the observers were moving their own fingers. Some scientists now believe that mirror neurons play a similar role in emotions, in which we mimic and even empathize with the emotions of others.[25]

Neuroscientists have also identified what they call emotional contagion. When we empathize with someone's emotion, it lights up the brain as though we'd felt the emotion ourselves. It's the reason that when one baby cries in the nursery, they all cry. It's not that the one baby has awakened the others (although that may be true). It's that the other babies quite literally feel his pain. Other studies have shown how an emotional contagion spreads through communities of people, so that happy people can spawn an epidemic of happy people around them.[26] The magnetism of a single leader, of course, can infect an entire group, for good and for bad. In a remarkable description of Apple in the mid-1980s, John Sculley recalls the force of personality that Steve Jobs radiated throughout the firm: "I couldn't explain what was going on when I arrived," Sculley recalled in *Odyssey*. "It was almost as if there were magnetic fields, some spiritual force, mesmerizing people; their eyes were just dazed. Excitement showed on everyone's face. It was nearly a cult environment."[27]

Fear is a strong catalyst, and visionaries are well known for blowing their tops. Jobs is famous for his expletive-laden rages. Rubbia would turn red and scream at his fellow scientists. When Walt Disney reviewed the work of his animators, their knees would shake like those of the cartoon characters they created. One time Roy Disney harangued a group of his brother's animators to stand up more often to Walt. "What the hell! Walt—is he some ogre?" Roy said (according to Don Peri's interview of animator Ben Sharpsteen). "Is he some tough prizefighter that you are afraid of? Are you a lot of dogs that stick your tails between your legs, because you're scared of Walt?" Replied one of them, "Roy, why do you blame us for being scared to death of Walt, when you're scared to death of him as well?"[28]

To be sure, fulminations are not uncommon among visionaries. But the remarkable thing is that beneath the fireworks, they seem to be able to stay cool themselves. When everyone else is falling apart around them, in other words, visionaries keep their heads. This doesn't mean that they can't turn as red as a beet. But it means that they can think clearly even under the most intense pressure. In fact, emotional, anxiety-provoking situations seem to clarify a visionary's thinking. But how do they do it?

When emotion overwhelms us, the amygdalae go into crisis mode.

Under pressure, they run screaming to the hypothalamus, which triggers the body's emergency response substance, corticotropin-releasing hormone (CRH), which triggers a cascade of fight-or-flight hormones. The amygdala also sends signals to the cardiovascular system, the muscles, and the gut. Norepinephrine suffuses the brain, setting your "nerves" on edge. Dopamine puts your muscles in readiness and heightens your vision and hearing.[29]

The worst result of this is that our working memory—the place where our cognition takes place—is literally short-circuited by the fireworks in our mind. We literally can't think straight. In *Emotional Intelligence,* Daniel Goleman relates an episode with which most of us can empathize: Marching in terror into a classroom in his freshman year in college, he sat down and opened a test for which he had not studied. "What strikes me most about the dreadful moment was how constricted my mind became," he writes. "I did not spend the hour in a desperate attempt to patch together some semblance of answers to the test. I did not daydream. I simply sat fixated on my terror, waiting for the ordeal to finish."[30]

Emotions like that can build in a feedback loop, like a microphone placed next to a live amp. There's no doubt that visionaries suffer their moments of shock. But visionaries don't collapse into an emotional pile. They can't.

Fortunately, the antidote to the amygdala seems to be the cerebral cortex, and particularly the left prefrontal lobe. While the right prefrontal lobe seems to house fear, aggression, and other negative emotions, the left prefrontal lobe can extinguish a flash of panic or even the accelerating cycle of emotional distress. Goleman calls the left frontal lobe the "neural thermostat." If you've ever been startled by a police or fire siren and then instantly realized that it was merely an emergency vehicle making its way past you, you've felt the spike of heat from the amygdala, followed by a reciprocating flash of cognition that douses the fire.

In some of us, the ability to put out the fire in more complex issues—such as the bank that refuses to renew the loan, the supplier that holds up shipment until it receives cash, the new product that flops and is flogged by the press, the trusted friend found conspiring with the other side—gives us the ability to coolly assess the situation and make the changes needed to survive. That, in a nutshell, is the aspect of emotional intelligence that visionaries use to endure. It makes them leaders as well.

You can't help but feel the personal power of a true visionary. You can't stand in a garage with Jobs explaining how it all began, or hang out on a houseboat with Branson discussing his dreams, or find your way deep underground with Rubbia talking in a stream of metaphors and simile, or wait on the tarmac with Burt Rutan shading his eyes from the sun—as I have—without feeling it.

The word is charisma. It is an overused word, I agree, but hard to avoid. Some experts say charisma has something to do with speaking well. Others attribute it to body language. Some suggest a confident smile. Others say if you want to be charismatic, dress well. "Animal magnetism" is also sometimes evoked. (That's a term postulated in the eighteenth century by Franz Mesmer—hence "mesmerize"—based on the idea that a magnetic fluid [or life force] builds so strongly in some people that it can be channeled, through the laying-on of hands, to others. That suggestion was quashed by a French royal commission set up by Louis XVI to examine the theory in 1784. Since it wasn't good enough for Louis XVI, we'll let it rest as well.)

Brain science, however, offers some real insight. In *Strangers to Ourselves,* psychology professor Timothy Wilson says that the human personality resides in two places—the "adaptive unconscious," which is what we are beneath the skin, and in our "constructed selves." The constructed self bears little resemblance to the unconscious self, he says, noting, "The constructive self consists of life stories that they have created about themselves—narratives that they tell about their past, present, and future, including self-theories and beliefs," adding that "people are forced to construct theories about their own personalities from other sources, such as what they learn from their parents, their culture, and, yes, ideas about who they prefer to be."[31]

What's particularly interesting, he notes, is that while we are familiar with the "constructed selves" we build, we are less familiar with our *real* selves. In one study, in which the participants (and their friends) were asked to rate their level of agreeableness and conscientiousness, the participants rated themselves higher than their friends rated them.

But the self-deception doesn't stop there. We also are poor at predicting how we might react to a particular situation. Wilson cites one study in which students are asked whether they will purchase a flower as part of a campus charity drive in the upcoming week. About 83 percent said they would, but only 43 percent actually did. But when they asked the students how many people overall would buy a flower, they replied 56 percent, which was closer to the 43 percent figure. We really are, as Wilson says, "strangers to ourselves."[32]

While Wilson notes that people whose life stories bear *no* resemblance to their actual lives end up in mental hospitals, he is struck by how many of us lead dualistic lives. Wilson quotes from Richard Russo's novel *Straight Man:* "The truth is, we never know for sure about ourselves . . . only after we've done a thing do we know what we'll do . . . Which is why we have spouses and children and parents and colleagues and friends, because someone has to know us better than we know ourselves."[33]

And visionaries? I would suggest they are not a blurry image, not a waffling story, not a constructed self. Certainly, visionaries may be duplicitous, shallow, deceptive—and you may love them or hate them—but they are authentic, the real thing. That's where their magnetism comes from.

"This above all: to thine own self be true," wrote Shakespeare. "And it must follow as the night the day. Thou canst not then be false to any man." Daniel Goleman puts this in a modern frame: Emotional intelligence, he says, allows people to act "in accord with their deepest feelings and values, no matter what the social consequences."[34]

In *A New Earth,* philosopher Eckhart Tolle notes, "In a world of role-playing personalities, those few people who don't project a mind-made image . . . but function from the deeper core of their being, those who do not attempt to appear more than they are but are simply themselves, stand out as remarkable and are the only ones who truly make a difference in the world."[35]

Walt Disney has been described by those who worked with him as a storyteller, a showman, a born leader. He was called charming, captivating, a good father. He was restless, driven, demanding, and—even among those who loved and respected him—rude, ruthless, and aloof. He was even called a genius. But nowhere among the hundreds of interviews of Disney animators and employees do you hear the people who worked with Walt describing him as a visionary.

It's almost as if the word "visionary" grows *outside* the inner circle. It eclipses the person, making him or her more than mortal. "Walt was a common man and a Missouri farm boy with a very limited education," said Herb Ryman, a Disney art director and one of the very few admitted into Disney's inner circle of friends. "Walt was not a deity. Walt was not superman. Walt was just a regular, live, flesh-and-blood person."[36]

And yet, we know there was something more about Walt.

Something mythic. Disney art director Ken Anderson recalled the time when he, Disney, and a few other studio people were invited to a grand soiree in Atlanta to celebrate the release of *Song of the South*. "The mayor made his entrance, but the decibel level in the room changed very little when he arrived," Anderson said. "There was still this hum of people talking and drinking and having a big time. Other important people came in. I had my back turned, and all of a sudden, there was dead silence. Walt's picture hadn't been published much in those times. This was 1946 and not many people knew what he looked like. He wasn't a big, imposing figure anyway. He came in with two or three other people, a couple who were known in the movies but they weren't big names. The whole place stopped, and I swear you could *feel* Walt in the room. We used to kid when we were doing *Bambi* about 'Man is in the forest.' We used that line for Walt. When Walt was around, you could *feel* him there."[37]

7

CHAPTER SEVEN

Luck

I took a book down from a shelf in my father's library and blew the dust from its pages. It was Julius Caesar's *War Commentaries,* this edition published when you could still buy a paperback for 75 cents—and written about 2,000 years before that. By chance I opened it to a page on which Caesar was describing his army's conquest of the German tribesmen.

Many of the Huns had been pacified, huddled in their deerskins within the Roman compounds. But now Caesar's army had crossed the Rhine in pursuit of one of the holdouts, the fierce chieftain Ambiorix. To capture Ambiorix, Caesar sent Lucius Minucius Bacillus ahead of the main army, commanding him to move stealthily and without campfires. As it turned out, Bacillus completed his march more quickly than thought possible, and took the camp of Ambiorix by complete surprise.

It was enough to make Caesar sit back and reflect. "In war, as in everything else," he wrote, "fortune plays a very great part. Bacillus was extremely lucky in catching Ambiorix's men completely off his guard . . ."

Yet that wasn't the end of the story. Ambiorix's men were able to hold off the Romans long enough for Ambiorix to escape into the woods on horseback. "It was by an extremely great stroke of luck that Ambiorix himself escaped with his life, after losing all the military equipment he had with him," wrote Caesar. "So by pure luck he was first of all brought into danger, and then liberated from it."[1]

You can't dismiss it. Visionaries are lucky. They've received all the breaks that luck bestows, and not just once, but again and again.

Suppose Orville Wright had died of the scarlet fever he had contracted in 1896, when he was twenty-five. Would Wilbur have built the flying machine by himself? Not likely. Suppose Andrew Carnegie had not read about the new blast furnaces that were revolutionizing the German steel industry, and, furthermore, hadn't found the financing to bring one back to the United States. Would he have transformed the steel business in America? Not likely. Carnegie Hall would not exist.

Suppose Walt Disney's cartoon business in Kansas City had been a modest success rather than a flop, and he had stayed there in the Midwest. Would he have forfeited the chance to meet the great animators who were shuffling around Southern California looking for someplace to go? Probably so.

I remember sitting with Michael Dell in his freshman dorm room at the University of Texas as he described how he started his computer company there in the 1970s. His parents were dead set against his obsession with computers—they wanted him to become a doctor.

The phone in his dorm room rang one day. It was his parents. They were in the lobby and on their way up. Dell hastily gathered the computer parts that were scattered all over his room (he had placed an ad in the Austin newspapers and had been happily building computers for his customers) and hid them in the bathtub. Well, Dell's mom went into the bathroom and didn't even pull aside the curtain (to the relief of the perspiring Michael)![2]

But suppose she had. Suppose Mrs. Dell had pulled that shower curtain aside, found her son's stash of computer parts, and raised hell. Dell might have given up and gone to medical school. Dell might have been your family doctor today.

I won't go on with the possibilities. It just underscores the *It's a Wonderful Life* aspect of our everyday lives.

In the film *Sliding Doors,* Gwyneth Paltrow's character has just lost her job at a public relations firm. As she descends into the subway, she hesitates as she steps around a girl playing with a doll. From then on the story splits down two paths. In one, the momentary hesitation causes her to miss her train. She hails a taxi instead. A thug grabs her handbag. She fights back and winds up in the hospital. In the second scenario, she *doesn't* hesitate, *does* catch the train, gets home early, and finds her boyfriend in the sack with his former flame. In the end, Paltrow's bifurcated character achieves romance and success. (You'll have to get the film to see how it all turns out.)

That's Hollywood. But in this case, Hollywood is a lot like life. "A lot of what happens to us—success in our careers, in our investments, and in our life decisions, both major and minor—are as much the result of random factors as the result of skill, preparedness, and hard work," writes Leonard Mlodinow in *The Drunkard's Walk: How Randomness Rules Our Lives.* "The outline of our lives, like the candle's flame, is continuously coaxed in new directions by a variety of random events that, along with our responses to them, determine our fate."[3]

This is particularly true of Thomas Kuhn's paradigm-busting moments: Most scientific discoveries are made by luck. In fact, some science historians argue that *all* scientific discoveries of merit are made through luck (otherwise they would be merely incremental, and not transformational). Pasteur, Jenner, Curie, Fleming, Edison—they all stumbled onto their epiphanies. That's why visionaries keep their eyes open for luck. For without that attitude, they might not notice their lucky break in the first place.

One famous visionary you may not have heard of was Luigi Galvani. But his story is worth retelling. Galvani was an anatomist at the University of Bologna. One breezy day in 1786 he was experimenting with static electricity. At the same time, he had strung together a few frog legs for another experiment near an iron balustrade. A gust of wind blew the legs into the iron. A spark arced, the legs began to dance, and Galvani (we can presume) smacked his forehead in glee: He had just discovered that electricity is the substance that triggers our muscles and nerves. And that's why we still say that something is *galvanizing*—or that we have been *galvanized* into action.

Feeling lucky is like that. It's like the hair floating up on your neck preceding a bolt from the blue. Sometimes people wake up feeling lucky.

"I should have stayed in camp that morning—but I didn't," wrote Donald Johanson in *Lucy: The Beginnings of Mankind.* Johanson is not just a paleoanthropologist; he is also the bone hunter who made one of the great finds of anthropology, that of *Australopithecus afarensis,* aka Lucy, the famous 3.2-million-year-old hominid. "I felt a strong subconscious urge to go with Tom [Gray, his graduate-student companion], and I obeyed it," he continued. "I wrote a note to myself in my daily diary: 'Nov. 30, 1974. To Locality 162 with Gray in AM. Feel good.'"[4]

Johanson was camped at the time in a wasteland of bare rock, gravel, and sand in Awash, Nairobi. With him was graduate student Gray. "As a paleoanthropologist—one who studies the fossils of human ancestors—I am superstitious," Johanson continued. "Many of us are, because the work we do depends on a great deal of luck. The fossils we study are extremely rare, and quite a few distinguished paleoanthropologists have gone a lifetime without finding a single one. I am one of the more fortunate . . . I know I'm lucky, and I don't try to hide it. That is why I wrote 'feel good' in my diary. When I got up that morning I felt it was one of those days when you should press your luck. One of those days when something terrific might happen."

In this case, his intuition was right; it was the day that he found Lucy—or at least a good portion of her diminutive skeleton—in an isolated gulley.

To a greater extent than most people realize, luck is what separates life's winners from the losers. Economist W. Brian Arthur noted the prominence of luck in an article he wrote for *Scientific American:* "In the real world, if several similar-sized firms entered a market together, small, fortuitous events—unexpected orders, chance meetings with buyers, managerial whims—would help determine which ones received early sales, and over time, which came to dominate. Economic activity is [determined] by individual transactions that are too small to foresee, and these small "random" events could accumulate and become magnified by positive feedbacks over time."[5]

Nassim Nicholas Taleb agrees that luck, not perseverance or any skill, is what accounts for the lion's share of success. Look at any study of millionaires, he says, and you will see that they share such traits as courage, risk taking, optimism, and so on. Then, he says, look across the road at people who never achieved success. "The graveyard of failed persons will be full of people who shared the following traits: courage, risk taking, optimism, et cetera. Just like the population of millionaires . . . There may be some differences in skills, but what truly separates the two is for the most part a single factor: luck. Plain luck."[6]

In other words, it was only luck that saved Michael Dell, by keeping his mother from nosing around in his shower; Orville Wright, by giving him a brother, Wilbur; and Walt Disney, by summoning up a failure in Kansas so that he would go to Los Angeles, where fame awaited him. But if luck is all that stands between those autographing their business best sellers and those moldering anonymously in the grave—what can we do to harness it?

Have we no say over our fates? Are we the victims of circumstances out of our control? Why am I reminded of the Old Testament admonition, as served up by Woody Allen: "Whosoever shall not fall by the sword or by famine shall fall by pestilence . . . so why bother shaving?"[7]

To be sure, luck doesn't come from personal planning. In fact, by definition, pure luck doesn't have anything to do with what we do. For instance, many people think they can improve their chances of winning a coin-toss by practicing.[8]

In 1975, a group of Yale undergraduates were asked to predict the results of 30 coin tosses. One-quarter said their performance would be hampered by a distraction, and 40 percent said that their performance would improve with practice. For the record, you absolutely, positively cannot improve your chances of betting on the flip of a coin, no matter how much sweat or study you put into it (variations of the same study proved the same point). Coins do not have a memory of what they did on the last flip, nor do roulette wheels. It's completely random, and we can't do anything to change that.

But a lot of life is not purely random. It falls into patterns. The brain is alert to patterns, and if you are alert to your brain, then good fortune may not necessarily follow, but your chances (unlike those of a coin landing heads up) will improve. Fossil hunters, for instance, don't wander the earth at random. They go where volcanoes wreaked havoc millions of years ago. They look for places where ash fell like powdered cement, and, in the rain, preserved bones and bodies for millions of years. That's how they improve their luck.

It's no different if you are looking for people to staff your high-tech start-up. Steve Jobs credits much of his success to the garages in his neighborhood, filled with fathers on the weekends tinkering with electronics. Steve Wozniak and other founders of the personal computer revolution grew up in the same fertile crescent. No place on earth had more geeks in one place than the 20 miles surrounding their homes.

Similarly, Wall Street has been the place to find financial talent. Los Angeles is where the stars are found. If you want to meet the world's best charcuterie chefs, go to France, not Gary, Indiana. When asked why he robbed banks, Willie Sutton famously replied, "Because that's where the money is."

In terms of being in the right place, can you imagine being in an Apple store somewhere, bending over the screen of an iPad, and then finding Steve Jobs standing there when you turn around? "So, how do you like it?" he says, crossing his arms. Or you're on a Virgin 747 over the Atlantic and Richard Branson strolls down the aisle and sits with you for a Pims and a chat.

The same stroke of luck hit the Motown Museum in Detroit a few years ago. The tour buses were lined up out front. The tourists were filling the house, where they inspected the framed photos of the Motown stars and the costumes, props, and programs that accompanied the shows.

Suddenly there was a commotion. Everyone seemed to be drawn by a magnet toward one end of the museum. The crowd packed in tighter and tighter. The whispers rose quickly to astonished cries. And there, standing in the middle of the admiring throng, with a smile that spanned from ear to ear, was Berry Gordy Jr., the founding father of Motown. The man! It was an instant love fest.[9]

But if lucky means being at the Motown Museum just when Berry Gordy happens to stroll through the door, it also says a lot about the founding of Motown itself.

Berry and his second wife, Raynoma, started the music empire in a one-room apartment in Detroit back in 1958. Berry was a songwriter with one big hit under his belt, "Reet Petite," sung by Jackie Wilson, and another, "Lonely Teardrops," in the works. He had a keen and intuitive ear for what would make a hit record.

Raynoma was a classically trained musician who could play piano, sing, and, most important, arrange music and write lead sheets. First they started the Rayber Music Writing Company. When they had some success, but found that most of their profits were going to the record label, they did the logical thing: They started their own label.

"Enter Marv Johnson," Raynoma wrote in *Berry, Me, and Motown*, "and we got lucky." Marv Johnson had not only a remarkable voice but a song in his pocket that they were certain would be a hit. It would cost $800 to get it recorded, and fortunately (once again) Berry Gordy's family agreed to loan them the money. Released in January 1959, the record, fortunately, *was* a hit.[10]

That summer Berry and Raynoma found a house for sale. It had a big cinder-block room in back that the previous owner, a photographer, had used as a studio. That's where they set up their recording equipment. "Hitsville," as the house was dubbed, became the place where, for the next dozen years, most of Motown's hits— some 100 of them—would be made.

But what was really lucky was that Berry and Raynoma had landed in the middle of what could be considered a fertile crescent of musical talent. Songwriters began to pour in over the threshold— people like Janie Bradford ("Money") and Brian Holland, Lamont

Dozier, and Eddie Holland ("Baby Love," "Heat Wave"). Extraordinary nightclub musicians appeared, like James Jamerson on bass, Benny Benjamin on drums, and Joe Messina on guitar. And of course, there was Motown's roster of singers. "They were just the kids in the neighborhood," Berry told me as I sat with him in Motown's original recording studio: Diana, Martha, Smokey, Marvin, and more. Detroit, it turned out, was a gold mine of talent.

Luck also takes *timing*—being in the right place at the right time. The problem with timing is that while we have some control over being in the right place, we don't have much control over being there at the right time. "We can move in space exactly as we please," notes Stefan Klein in *The Secret Pulse of Time*. "Time, by contrast, appears to carry us along with it."[11]

But what's interesting about paradigm shifts and innovation is that they often come in clumps. In *Knowledge, Morality, and Destiny,* biologist Julian Huxley notes, "Exceptionally gifted individuals are able to realize their talent effectively not at a constant or even approximately constant rate in time, nor in a uniform extension in different areas, but in bursts; and . . . these bursts are related to the stage of development of the culture into which the potential geniuses are born."[12]

This is why, he continued, discoveries and ideas are often and perhaps usually made independently by more than one person at about the same time. When you think about it, it's true. The Wright brothers were surrounded by glider experts, and several were getting close to making an airplane. The same is true about Jobs and the PC revolution. Apple was hardly the first PC, although it became one of the most successful.

But why is it that disparate groups of people are working on the same idea at the same time? Thomas Kuhn says this happens because a paradigm is often preceded by a crisis of confidence in the old idea. "Galileo's contribution to the study of motion depended closely upon difficulties discovered in Aristotle's theory by scholastic critics," says Kuhn. "Newton's new theory of light and color originated in the discovery that none of the existing pre-paradigm theories would account for the length of the spectrum."[13]

In other words, there's a lot of grumbling before a paradigm breaks loose. Critics become bolder. If a visionary is in the right place, and recognizes that the general grumbling likely portends a change, they could likely become "lucky" as well. Think back to Diane von Furstenberg, who couldn't find a simple, fashionable dress amidst the hippie clothing and the pantsuits of the early 1970s. Or Jeff Hawkins, with the PalmPilot, exploiting the dissatisfaction that people had with handhelds at the time.

I remember speaking once to Paul Orfalea, the founder of Kinko's. Orfalea was severely dyslexic and a poor student. He decided that the only thing he could do in life was be a peddler. So, while a student at the University of California at Santa Barbara, he placed notebooks and pencils for sale on the sidewalk leading between the classrooms. Next he leased a former hamburger shack and rolled a copier attached to an extension cord onto the sidewalk, charging four cents for a copy. That became the first little Kinko's store.

Business was good. One store led to another. Before long, Kinko's (Orfalea's nickname for his curly red hair) was spreading coast to coast. Why? While it had something to do with the convenience of Kinko's stores, which were open 24 hours a day, it had a lot more to do with Orfalea's fortunate *timing:* The country was experiencing a massive wave of corporate layoffs in the early 1990s, people were starting their own businesses, and Kinko's was open 24 hours a day. Kinko's was not only a place to make copies, but also a place to meet other fledgling entrepreneurs (many of them recently downsized out of their jobs). In 2004 Orfalea sold the company to FedEx for $2.4 billion.[14]

Berry Gordy arrived at the right time too. When the Motown kids boarded a bus for their first tours into the South, the groups played segregated halls. A rope down the middle of the room divided the races, with the white kids on one side clapping to the upbeat, and the black kids on the other clapping to the downbeat. But the times were rapidly changing. Mainstream radio was finally ready for black singers and soul music. Newly minted six-transistor radios were the iPods of their day. Once again, the vision met the flood tide.

No matter how much pressure there is for change, of course, it can happen only when technology is good enough to drill down deep enough to reach it. And then you have a gusher. That was certainly true in the case of the personal computer. Until Xerox PARC developed the graphic user interface and the mouse, the personal computer was a hobbyist's game. But once Jobs and Bill Gates snatched the idea from Xerox and developed it, personal computers arrived for the everyman.

The Wright brothers were also fortunate in that the technology of flight had gradually advanced so that someone somewhere was going to make an airplane that flew. Their flier may have been the product of these two men, but it embodied all the trial and error of the previous 40 years of glider flying. On top of that, the internal combustion engine had just barely reached the point that it could crank out enough horsepower per pound to make a flight mechanically feasible.

"If the Wright brothers had been a generation older, it is not at all certain that they would have avoided the stumbling blocks of those who were working in the second half of the 19th century," says Peter Jakab in *Visions of a Flying Machine*. "The Wrights were especially talented, to be sure, but there is no reason to believe their genius operated in a vacuum, and that they would have invented the airplane no matter when they took up the problem."[15]

When paradigms burst upon us, the time is ripe not only for the few who have created the paradigm, but for everyone else who happens to be standing by. Paradigm-making moments, Kuhn reminds us, are always followed by years of what he calls "mopping up." Huxley puts it this way: "Once a science has reached the stage of having a coherent theoretical basis, it will inevitably proceed . . . to make further discoveries and further extension of its theory."[16]

That's why commercial products often follow scientific break-throughs by about 20 years or so. Ford built his first car some 20 years or so after the invention of the internal combustion engine; Jobs and Wozniak built their first PC 20 years after the first transistor was made. "First movers," in other words (and contrary to the mantra of the "New Economy" of the late 1990s), very often do not prevail. This means you don't need to *deliver* the paradigm to mop up quite successfully in its aftermath. You don't even need to be the first mover. Just be clever enough to make off with the flotsam of the paradigm after it has crashed upon the shore.

So persistence drives visionary success. If you aren't out there flipping coins, after all, you'll never get one to land in your favor. That means take an occasional break in your pursuit, change direction perhaps, but as Churchill remarked, never, ever give in.

"You start by having something in your mind and you say, 'Hey, maybe this will work,'" Carlo Rubbia explained in a BBC interview. "If it doesn't, well, you forget about it, and say, 'Let's look at something else.' Then two days later you get it again and say, 'Hey, it's still okay, maybe we do have a way of getting through this thing. Maybe it will work.' Then you get some number back that looks horrible and say, 'Well, it will not work after all' . . . So you drive your way painfully through it a number of different ways . . ."[17]

I asked a friend, whose brother is a very successful entrepreneur, how he hit the big time. The fellow isn't smarter than anyone else. In fact, he was fired from a job doing just what he's doing now—and what he's doing now has made him rich, so rich, in fact, that he has a driver, maids, chefs, and a waterfront estate in Connecticut. His sister explained that when her brother started out, his business was like a boat floating among many competitors. At first there were a dozen boats. Then a big storm blew through. He held on, and when it was over, a half-dozen boats were left. Then there was another storm. He held on again, and there were three boats. And then another storm, and he was the only boat left. And that's how he got so big. It was just a matter of grit and determination. That's what it takes.

"In the twenty years I have spent in this business, I have weathered many storms. It has been far from easy sailing," Disney said grimly to his employees in a memo circulated during the bitter union strike at the studio in 1941. "It has required a great deal of hard work, struggle, determination, confidence, faith, and above all, unselfishness . . . I have had a stubborn, blind confidence in the cartoon medium, a determination to show the skeptics that the animated cartoon is deserving of a better place . . . that it was more than a novelty." He continued, "I have been flat broke twice in twenty years. Once in 1923 before I came to Hollywood I was so broke I went for three days without eating a meal, and I slept on some old canvas and chair cushions in an old rat-trap of a studio for which I hadn't paid any rent for months. Again in 1928 my brother Roy and I had everything we owned at that time mortgaged. It wasn't much but it was all we had."[18]

Most visionaries have fought their way through similar storms. Though it may look like luck from afar, on closer examination it's most often a white-knuckled hold on the gunwales that has kept them alive.

"Keep marching forward," says Mlodinow, "because the best

news is that since chance does play a role, one important factor in success is under our control: the number of at-bats, the number of chances taken, the number of opportunities seized. For even a coin weighted toward failure will sometimes land on success."[19]

You rarely read news stories about people with visionary ideas who've failed, unless they have been identified as a visionary before the failure. Otherwise, each is simply another anonymous flop, slipping silently beneath the waves. But recently, the story of a visionary who did fail made the pages of newspapers and Web sites around the world. In his case, the story involved fluorescent piglets, green cats, and the Nobel Prize.

In the late 1980s, a biochemist named Douglas Prasher received a three-year, $200,000 grant from the American Cancer Society to try to clone the gene for green fluorescent protein from *Aequorea victoria,* a species of Pacific Ocean jellyfish that glows bright green under ultraviolet light. The fluorescent material, it was believed, could be injected into other cells so that one might watch events that hitherto had been invisible—like the development of nerve cells in the brain or the spread of cancer cells.

Prasher, who graduated with a PhD in biochemistry from Ohio State University and who had previously worked with the jellyfish at the University of Georgia and then at the Woods Hole Oceanographic Institution, set to work. By the end of his three-year stint, he had succeeded. Like any good scientist, he shared his findings, passing his results, and some of the cloned material, to Martin Chalfie, a geneticist at Columbia University.

Prasher was set to do more when he was informed that he had failed to attain tenure at Woods Hole and would have to leave. He applied to the National Institutes of Health for funding but was turned down. He finally landed a job with the U.S. Department of Agriculture as a population geneticist at its Otis Plant Protection

Center on Cape Cod, Massachusetts, and was later transferred to its Plant Germplasm Quarantine & Biotechnology Laboratory in Beltsville, Maryland. While Prasher was bouncing from job to job, leaving him no time for *Aequorea victoria,* Chalfie at Columbia was making steady progress: He had been able to splice the material into *E. coli* and then into the roundworm *C. elegans.* Sure enough, the protein inside glowed green, proving that it could be used as a tag in a variety of ways.

Things got progressively worse for Prasher. Funding was cut at the Beltsville, Maryland, lab. Bravely, Prasher bounced from there to AZ Technology in Huntsville, Alabama. Then he lost that job in another round of cuts.

Meanwhile, the fluorescent protein was becoming recognized as what *Science Daily* called "one of the most important tools used in contemporary bioscience." With it, researchers would be able to follow nerve cell damage during Alzheimer's disease and watch insulin-producing beta cells as they are created in the pancreas. They could tag the cells of the brain as well, in a rainbow of colors.

The protein had become a pop culture item as well, much to the mortification of serious scientists. A team of Chinese researchers created a fluorescent sow that gave birth to a litter of green glowing pigs. A South Korean created a cat that glowed as green as a firefly, and had three green kittens. A conceptual artist, Eduardo Kac, entered a glowing green rabbit in a French art show. He was rebuffed ("Glowing Bunny Sparks International Controversy" screamed the headline in *Biology News*). But Kac had his supporters. Among them was Harvard art history professor Frank Fehrenbach, who maintained that even Leonardo da Vinci had toyed around with animal aesthetics, once attaching wings, horns, and a beard to a living lizard—and then covering him with quicksilver.[20]

The climax came in October 2008, when Chalfie, along with Osamu Shimomura of the Marine Biology Laboratory and Boston

Medical School, and Roger Y. Tsien of the University of California at San Diego, won the Nobel Prize "for the discovery and development of the green fluorescent protein, GFP." (Shimomura was the first person to isolate GFP from the jellyfish, Tsien learned how to give the cells different colors, and Chalfie demonstrated its use as a luminous genetic tag.)[21]

But there was no mention of Douglas Prasher. The Nobel can be shared among a maximum of three recipients, and Prasher hadn't made the cut. When interviewed by National Public Radio's *Inside Edition,* Prasher said that he had been unable to find a job in science, his life savings had run out, and he was now working as a courtesy shuttle-bus driver for Bill Penney Toyota in Huntsville, Alabama.[22]

In their Nobel speeches in Stockholm that winter, all three men thanked Prasher profusely (a welcome relief, considering that the Nobels are notorious for leaving out significant contributors to scientific achievement). "Douglas Prasher's work was critical and essential for the work we did in our lab," said Chalfie with great generosity. "They could've easily have given the prize to Douglas and the other two and left me out."

"I'm really happy for them," replied Prasher, adding that in the face of his tough circumstances, withholding the glowing material from Chalfie would not have been the right thing to do.[23]

An honest and talented man, Douglas Prasher. He could have been a contender. He just ran out of luck.

8

CHAPTER EIGHT

The Limits of Vision

Pixar is one of the most famous Hollywood brands nowadays, but at the time I interviewed Jobs in 1995, *Toy Story* was still a few weeks from release and Pixar meant nothing to most people, including me. Even Jobs didn't realize how the heavens were about to open—how *Toy Story* and Pixar would not only make him a billionaire, but lift him into a second life of fame and fortune beyond his wildest dreams.

Pixar was founded by Edwin Catmull, a man who had hoped to become a Disney animator—until he realized he couldn't draw. Undeterred, Catmull invented a way for a computer to draw realistic three-dimensional shapes as well as convincing textures (this while pursuing graduate studies at the University of Utah). Shortly after graduating in 1974, Catmull was hired by Dr. Alexander Schure (an entrepreneur who had founded the New York Institute of Technology) to start a computer graphics lab that focused on computer animation. As David A. Price relates in *The Pixar Touch,* Catmull hired a few other computer animation savants, and shortly thereafter, the group went to work in their makeshift workshop, which happened to be a former four-car garage and chauffeurs' quarters on Long Island's North Shore. Thus, the seeds for Pixar were planted.[1]

Five years later, having improved the fluidity of his computer animation, and having assembled a small but talented group of collaborators (including Alvy Ray Smith, a brilliant electrical engineering grad from Stanford), Catmull received a call from none other than George Lucas, who had just made *Star Wars*. Lucas needed a team to create special effects, like spaceships and lightsaber blades, for his films. When George Lucas calls, you jump. And that's what Catmull and many of his colleagues at New York Tech did. They moved from Long Island to the sprawling Northern California campus of Lucasfilm.

By the fall of 1982 Catmull's group had wowed critics with the special effects for *Star Trek II: The Wrath of Khan*. More important, Catmull met a twenty-six-year-old Disney animator by the name of John Lasseter. Catmull was impressed: *a real Disney animator!* But Lasseter's situation at Disney was far less than sanguine: He had been developing his own animation project, called "The Brave Little Toaster," at the studios. But the project had been canceled—and Lasseter, seen by the stodgy Disney bureaucracy as a hyperactive thorn in its side—had been fired. *Even better,* exclaimed Catmull, urging Lasseter to join him immediately at Lucasfilm.

With Lasseter onboard, Pixar began to make several short, computer-generated films. The first (so reminiscent, in its fumbling attempt to master the new technology, of the early Walt Disney cartoons) was a two-minute film about a boy and a bee. First shown at a convention of computer graphics enthusiasts in 1984, it received sustained applause.

But before Pixar could evolve any further, disaster struck: George Lucas had lost a lot of money in two expensive flops—his marriage, which ended in divorce, and his latest film, *Howard the Duck,* which had laid an egg at the box office. Desperate for cash, Lucas decided to sell Pixar's proprietary 3-D machine, the Pixar Image Computer.

And so Lucas peddled Pixar to Siemens—which imagined the computer as a complement to its CAT scanners. And to Hallmark—which saw it as a conduit between its artists and the printing presses. And to General Motors—which thought it could use Pixar to aid in automobile design. And to Philips Electronics—which would use the Pixar machine as an adjunct to its MRI scanners.

But in the end, nobody wanted Pixar. Every candidate dropped out. And then, in the summer of 1985, an unlikely suitor stepped forward: Steve Jobs. He offered $10 million. Lucas wanted $30 million.[2] Neither side would budge. Steve waited. A few months later, when it was clear that nobody else would step forward, Lucas accepted Jobs's $10 million offer. Steve Jobs now owned Pixar.

Visionaries sometimes seem to possess a crystal ball. Warren Buffett is called the "Oracle of Omaha" because his predictions (manifested through his stock purchases) have made him one of the wealthiest men in the world. Disney has been credited with enormous foresight as well. He not only predicted the success of the feature cartoon but also delighted the world with Disneyland and Disney World. Obviously, Steve Jobs also has this gift. He's made a number of stunning calls, from the original Apple to the Mac to the iPod to the iPhone, all the way up to the astounding success of the iPad.

But can visionaries really see into the future? Above and beyond their gifts of intuition and visualization, do they have brains that are wired somehow for prognostication—for peering down the long corridor of time and seeing what's coming?

If you asked most neuroscientists to describe the primary function of the human brain, they wouldn't say it's a calculating machine, or a dreaming machine, or even a communication machine. Most of them would say that the brain is a *prediction* machine. Watch a child put one block on top of another, then another on top of that, then another on top of that. A fifth block goes on top, and the pile begins to lean. What will happen next? It will fall. Suppose you have been burned twice by your boss, who takes your best ideas and presents them to his boss as his own. Now you are sitting down with your boss once again. What do you think will happen *this time* with your ideas?

Indeed, the brain is a prediction machine. It's the only way we could have survived: When we glanced at the furry beast with the big teeth we didn't have to puzzle over whether to run for the cave. We did it. These first impressions, or "thin slice judgments," are thought to be part of our primitive, instinctive arsenal for survival.

The mechanism behind this ability is pattern recognition. The brain recognizes a particular scenario, runs it against similar patterns in its memory, and reacts. Patterns are necessary for two reasons: The brain is relatively slow (much slower than a computer chip, for instance), and second, the working memory of the brain is limited.

As I noted earlier, we can remember about five to seven things simultaneously (that's why we divide phone numbers into three and four sequences, and assemble letters into words, and words into sentences). Patterns (even the sequence of actions we repeat to start the car in the morning) relieve the brain of thinking these problems through from scratch. We don't consume much computing power when we are merely comparing patterns. It is, dare I say it, a no-brainer.[3]

Some scientists believe that the right side of the brain seems to handle facts, and the left side handles patterns. So from infancy onward we are occupied with shuffling the elements of the world from the right to the left. Pile the blocks too high and they tumble. Next time, stack them in shorter, neater rows. The neurotransmitter that facilitates pattern making is dopamine; scientists have found that the more dopamine they give to their lab subjects, the easier it is for them to form patterns from disparate materials.

The mastery of patterns allows us to go about our everyday lives. You don't think about what your feet are doing while you walk. And when you read, you don't have to ponder each word anew. Pattern reading also endows some of us with marvelous abilities. A typical game of chess offers 10^{120} possible moves. That's more than the number of particles in the visible universe (which is 10^{79}, if you haven't counted them lately), notes Steven Pinker in *How the Mind Works*. So how do chess masters do it? As we saw earlier, good players have some 1,000 patterns stored in their heads. Masters have more than 50,000.[4]

Stored patterns also let baseball sluggers hit balls out of the park. At 80–100 mph, a major-league pitch takes about 0.35 seconds to travel from the pitcher's hand to the catcher's mitt. Unfortunately for the batter, that's faster than the human body can react: It takes twenty milliseconds for the brain to respond to a sensory stimulus, several milliseconds for the visual information to travel from the retina to the visual cortex, *and* 0.25 seconds for the batter's muscles to initiate the swing. So how do sluggers routinely send balls into the bleachers? By using patterns—the pitcher's body language, the position of the players in the field, the sense of the catcher behind the plate—batters subconsciously predict where the ball will be thrown.[5]

Life, in fact, is a series of *anticipations*. We are constantly anticipating what will happen next. Pascal once remarked, "We almost never think of the present, and when we do, it is only to see what light it throws upon our plans for the future." Indeed, says neurologist Antonio Damasio, there is "a virtual nonexistence of the present, consumed as we are by using the past to plan what comes next . . ."[6] In other words, we are literally leaning forward into the future on the tips of our toes—taking what we know from the past, and tossing it over the blue horizon.

We pay a price, however, to enjoy these pattern-based predictive abilities. How so? Because the same patterns that help us predict the future are also the ones that lock us into the present. It all goes back to the structure of the brain.

The specialized circuits that anticipate our futures are found in the brain stem and hypothalamus (as well as in those two emotion/memory-generating structures, the amygdala and the hippocampus). This is where scientists believe the patterns take residence (perhaps in physically adjacent constellations of neurons). The problem with these preexisting patterns is that they often cause us to make senseless, knee-jerk decisions—without ever realizing it.

Suppose there are three bottles of wine on the menu. One is $10, one is $15, and one is $21. Which one would most people choose? The answer is the middle one. Why? Because most of us *don't know* what we want—until we see something in context. That's why HDTV salesmen will put the set they want to move in the middle price bracket. Setting context is a common price-setting ploy. In *Predictably Irrational,* for example, we mention a New York restaurant consultant who always works an expensive meal into the menu so that customers will feel better choosing a dish that is slightly less expensive. Cognitive scientists call this particular piece of irrational thinking the *relativity heuristic* (a heuristic is a "rule of thumb" that has been hardwired into the brain).[7]

On the other hand, suppose you had studied three wines

exhaustively, and then heard someone at the next table remark that they liked the $10 bottle of wine. Which would you choose? Most people would order the $10 bottle—simply because they've heard something good about it. (This is called the *availability heuristic* referring to the influence that recent information has over our decision making.) Consider this example: You exhaustively study the attributes of various HDTVs and on the way to the store, you hear something good about a particular brand. What you've studied goes out the window, and you buy that brand.

Most of these heuristics were first identified in the 1970s by a group of brilliant researchers led by Daniel Kahneman (who won the Nobel Prize in economics in 2002 for these insights into decision making) and his collaborator Amos Tversky, as well as Richard Thaler and Paul Slovic.[8]

What they discovered was that to quickly reduce complex decisions to simple ones, the human brain has created a number of rules. They are prepackaged, drive-through-window decisions that don't need any contemplation.

The findings of Kahneman and his collaborators have huge import (beyond the selection of wines and HDTVs). They raise the question of how *rational* people really are. Let's not forget that America's Founding Fathers were big fans of John Locke and the other thinkers of the Enlightenment, who believed that humans are rational beings. That was the premise underlying the idea of a democracy: Given the opportunity, people would weigh things rationally (with the frontal cortex rather than the amygdala) and arrive at *logical* decisions. Kahneman's studies revealed, however, that people are apt to skip rational thought and go directly to the hardwired rules of thumb.

We're not even aware of these heuristics, but they can rule our lives, and often in unpleasant ways. Take, for instance, the *representativeness heuristic:* If one thing is *similar* to another, then it probably is the *same* as another. Consider this question, posed by psychologist David Myers: Suppose you heard about someone who is short, slim, and likes to read poetry. Is this person an Ivy League classics professor, or a truck driver? The most probable response, and the one associated with the *representativeness heuristic,* would be the classics professor.

But think again: There are eight Ivy League Schools, with perhaps 20 classics professors at each (so, 160 professors). Arguably half of these professors are short and slim (80) and, of these, let's say more than half like poetry (50). On the other hand, there are some three and a half million truck drivers in the country. Even if just 1 in 10 is short and slim, and of those just 1 percent like to read poetry, the number of truck drivers in that group (3,500) would still be about 70 times larger than the group of classics professors.[9]

Here's another example, courtesy of Professor Myers: A man is twice-divorced, likes to hang around the country club bar, and can be frequently heard stating that his long hours of academic study would have been better used learning to be less quarrelsome with others. The individual was selected from a group of 30 engineers and 70 lawyers. So is he a lawyer or an engineer?

When asked, 80 percent of the students said he was a lawyer. That may have made some sense statistically. But then Myers turned the tables and stated that the man was actually drawn from a group of 70 engineers and just 30 lawyers. So who was he now? Despite the far greater statistical chance that the man was an engineer, 80 percent still said he was an lawyer—because the evidence *seemed* to point that way.[10]

The point here is that the brain likes patterns better than facts. And it's more than happy to fill in missing pieces. Give it three-quarters of a circle and it can supply the rest. That's a good thing. Otherwise, if we saw two people sitting in a convertible, we would wonder what happened to the lower part of their bodies. Children understand that when a cartoon character hides behind a tree, with a foot protruding from one side and the head out the other, the rest of the body in between has not disappeared. That ability helps us in life. But in some situations, the brain's compulsion to complete the missing parts leads to false conclusions. We call them stereotypes.

What's counterintuitive about stereotypes is how often we try to be included in them—as long as the stereotypes are good ones. In fact, convincing people to do things that place them in the right stereotype slots is what advertising is all about.

As we saw earlier, advertising genius Shirley Polykoff proclaimed that *blondes have more fun.* So women everywhere ran out and bought bottles of Clairol. Everyone wanted to be a blonde—so they would have more fun (or at least persuade other people they were having more fun).

Apple has cleverly pitted their Mac guy (very cool) against the stuffy and clueless PC guy. Who do we want to be? Mac, of course.

The car we drive identifies us as an urban sophisticate, an outdoorsman, a cowboy, an environmentalist, and so forth. Even the brand names help herd us into our favorite group. People who drive Subaru Foresters must be heading to the *forest,* of course; those who are in Jeep Wranglers must be heading to the *ranch;* Chevy Suburban people are heading for the *burbs;* and those in Malibus are heading to the *beach.*

Even the clothes we wear often have the labels on the *outside.* (Levi Strauss may have started the modern trend in 1890, when they moved the label on their blue jeans that designated the fit and fabric to the back pocket, so that it was visible on the retailers' shelves.)[11]

While we spend a good deal of our time trying to get in with the right crowd (or at least be identified with it), we are also often slotted unfairly by others. People who are tarred with a broad brush have to fight back against it: Bikers run charity events to remind us that they're not all a bunch of leather-clad toughs. The Special Olympics was formed to remind us that the handicapped are not without athletic skills and aspirations.

Obviously, racial prejudice is a form of representative bias. One glance and a person is rushed into a slot. The arrest of Henry Louis Gates Jr. at his Cambridge home is the recent poster child for this. One early afternoon, Gates, head of Harvard's W.E.B. Du Bois Institute for African and African American research, prolific author, and a black male, was pushing at his front door with another black male, his taxi driver, trying to get the jammed door open. He was returning home following a trip to China, where he had been filming a documentary. A woman walking by saw what she assumed was a break-in and called the police. A dispute ensued between Gates and the officer, and Gates was handcuffed and taken downtown, where he spent four hours in a cell while things were, to the extent possible, straightened out.[12]

Had the analytical mind been in control, this might not have happened. The analytical mind would have recognized that while there is some small connection between African American men and break-ins, it doesn't extend any further than that (or, more precisely, in the words of the psychologists, "A previously learned correlation, which is from a very small sample, does not generalize to the exception"). But the hardwired mind has been programmed, for the sake of survival, to jump to conclusions. The representation bias permeates our lives, and despite all the foresight it provides in some ways, it cripples us in so many more.

In *Predictably Irrational* Dan Ariely and I introduced readers to Salvador Assael, otherwise known as "The Pearl King." Back in the 1960s Salvador had access to a great many black pearls, brought up from the blue waters of Tahiti. But he had no customers. Black pearls had never been mass-marketed before and so, "no one really knew how much a black pearl was worth," he said.

But Assael, who had made a fortune in white pearls (and was therefore able to afford luxury homes around the world), realized that the price he placed on the black pearls at the beginning would probably set their price forever. And so he priced them high—sometimes more than a million dollars for a single strand. And you know what? Tahitian pearls were accepted as expensive gems.[13]

When we don't know what something is worth, we take our first exposure to the price as the benchmark, and go on from there. This is called "anchoring." We are very much like newly hatched goslings, scampering after the first parental figure they see—be it a cat or a person.[14]

Anchoring exerts an incredibly strong hold on us. In one experiment, Kahneman and Tversky asked subjects to spin a roulette wheel and, when it stopped, to write down the number. Then they asked the subjects how many African nations belong to the UN. Incredibly, the number of African nations always fell close to the number that was noticed on the wheel. So if the number was five on the wheel, for instance, they might have said five, six, or seven African nations, and if it was eight, they might have replied with seven, eight, or nine. Dan Ariely has performed a similar experiment, first asking the participants to write down the last two digits of their Social Security number, and then asking them to bid on various items. The bids correlated strongly with the digits of the Social Security number that the subjects had jotted down. The mere suggestion of a number, in other words, is enough to influence our thinking.[15]

If that seems implausible to you, consider this: When you ask the TV salesman how much a 50-inch LCD set with surround-sound costs, and he replies with a price, you don't go home and furtively tally the costs of the component parts. As sticker-shocked as you may be, you still take that price as the benchmark. Why should a TV sell at a certain price? Or a Tahitian pearl? Or a radio wave that interacts with your cell phone? The fact of the matter is that initial prices are generally arbitary, but once set, they shape not only what we are willing to pay for an item, but also what we are willing to pay for related items. In economic terms, *that* is the anchor.

In broader terms, we also anchor many aspects of our lives. A teacher says she likes our voice, and it sticks; we begin to consider a career on the stage. Someone comments favorably on our hair, and we wear it like that for a long time. We come to a conclusion about a political issue, and keep pounding that drum even when the facts have changed. In other words, repeated exposure to something increases our *familiarity* with it. Pretty soon (like a song played frequently enough) we accept it. Familiarity, in fact, does not breed contempt.

Neuroscientists believe that when we become familiar enough with something, the neurons in our brains establish that pattern. That neuron constellation may take some time and effort to come together, but once established, it is there for good. It is why, in *Liars, Lovers and Heroes,* neurologists Steven Quartz and Terrence Sejnowski say, "If you spend an hour or two a day for the next three weeks learning to play the piano, you will be altering the structure of your brain."[16] Once the pattern is set, the brain moves on to other things. Seen through an fMRI, the nucleus accumbens (which plays a critical role in reward and pleasure) goes dark and the participation of the emotionally charged amygdala eases up. Why? Because the response has now become automatic.[17] That's why, once we've learned a new tune, we can play it effortlessly, and why, once having adopted an idea, we tend to stick with it.

In an experiment that demonstrated this, researchers at Stanford University described two firefighters to a group of students: One firefighter was a *risk taker*—and was an excellent firefighter. The other was cautious—and was a mediocre firefighter. When asked to form a conclusion from the discussion, the students responded that *risk taking* leads to better firefighting.

For the second group of students, however, the researchers flipped the story, describing a *cautious* firefighter (who was excellent at his job), and a risk taker (who was a mediocre firefighter). What's the lesson in this? the researchers asked. The students responded that *caution* leads to better firefighting.

It's understandable that the students would come to this conclusion. But what's irrational is the way that the students clung to their conclusions: Even when they were told that the cases were fabricated, those who had said that risk taking makes for better firefighting stuck with it. And those who had championed cautious firefighters hung in with that conclusion as well.[18] That's not just "human nature"; it's the way the brain works: Once we've reached a conclusion, we are generally loath to change it. We've sealed it away in a lockbox.

Steve Jobs would seem to be the last person you'd expect to find in a lockbox. But once Jobs bought Pixar, Lasseter, Catmull, and Smith found that they could not get Jobs excited about Pixar's prospects as an animation maker. You can imagine Jobs listening to them intently, chewing on a macroveggie snack. You can imagine

Jobs nodding his head as they told him about some of their computer animation successes, like the short film *Andre and Wally B,* which brought a crowd of computer enthusiasts to its feet clapping a year earlier; or the overtures a Japanese publishing company was making about funding a full-length computer- animated feature with them. But in the end Jobs saw Pixar as a software and computer maker. They couldn't shake that idea out of Jobs's head. In fact, in buying Pixar, Jobs was not reflecting back to Disney's golden age of animation at all, but to his own glory days at Apple. "The whole thing has the same flavor as the personal computer industry in 1978," he told *BusinessWeek.* Not surprisingly, the official press release from Jobs read:

> The new firm has a product, the Pixar Image Computer, ready for market. Developed during the last three years at Lucasfilm Ltd., the Pixar Image Computer is over 200 times faster than conventional minicomputers at performing complex graphic and image computations. At these specialized tasks, the Pixar Image Computer will be introduced into the commercial and scientific markets within the next 90 days and will sell for approximately $125,000.[19]

It said nothing about animated films.

The problem is that when we get an idea into our heads, it often transforms itself from an *idea* into a *belief.* Ideas are like wet cement. Beliefs are what happens when the cement sets. At that point it's hard to change your mind about something. Kahneman and his colleagues noticed something else about ideas and beliefs. When we form a belief about something, we start to treat it like a physical possession. That's why we *hold* a belief, or *cling to* a belief, or even *inherit* a belief. That's why we sometimes say, "I don't *buy* that."[20]

We've learned quite a few things about material things—thanks to researchers. For instance, we've learned that the more we see of something the more we tend to like it. In one experiment, researchers flashed pictures in front of people so fast that some of them could not even be consciously absorbed. Then they showed the pictures at a more leisurely rate (and mixed in some new ones) and asked the subjects to indicate which images they liked best. The researchers found that the subjects liked the pictures they had already seen. Researchers call this the "mere exposure effect."[21] That's why advertisers pound ads repeatedly down our throats. It's why chain restaurants (you get the same meal coast to coast) thrive.

Researchers have also found that once we own something we generally value it more than its worth. That's why sellers generally demand more for a house or a car than the buyers think it's worth.[22] Finally, researchers have shown that the more money we sink into something, the less willing we are to give it up—even if we know that it's a lost cause. Just examine your own coat closet for instance, for clothing you've rarely worn, and probably will not, but hate to give up.

What goes for material things, Kahneman discovered, also goes for ideas. The more we think about a particular concept, the more we like it. The more we like it, the more we value it. The more we value it, the more we are willing to invest in it (for instance, by cherry-picking through evidence for facts that support it). Astonishingly, we do this even when we vaguely suspect it is wrong.

In one experiment that demonstrates this, researchers projected a picture that was completely out of focus onto a screen. The slide was then gradually brought into sharper and sharper focus. The participants were instructed to guess what the picture showed (a fire hydrant in one case), and write it down. Remarkably, the individuals who were the *first* to think they knew the identity of the picture (and write it down) were the *last* to correctly identify it. Why? Because rather than scratch through their initial opinion as the image became clearer and they were increasingly and obviously wrong, they clung to it. People who were among the last to make an identification were more successful—simply because their first choice had a better chance of being right.[23]

In the face of strong evidence to the contrary, then, people not only stick loyally to their original bet, they actually can feel more strongly that it was right.

So we anchor ourselves to our beliefs—regardless of the faulty logic behind the initial decision. And once we adopt that idea, we seek not only to protect it, but also to look for additional evidence to corroborate it. This is called the "cognitive bias." It's the compulsion of the brain—now that our neurons have settled comfortably into a network over an idea—to maintain it.

But how do we react when we receive information that is contrary to our cherished point of view? In an interesting experiment, researchers at Stanford University asked 151 students their views on capital punishment.[24] From this group they selected 24 students who were strongly supportive of capital punishment and saw it as a deterrent, and 24 students who were strongly against it.

The mixed groups were seated at a large table. Next they were asked to draw a card from a selection of cards and read it silently to themselves. The cards for each session were either a pro-death-penalty card:

Kroner and Phillip (1977) compared murder rates for the year before and the year after adoption of capital punishment in 14 states. In 11 of the 14 states, murder rates were lower after adoption of the death penalty. This research supports the deterrent effect of the death penalty.

or an anti-death-penalty card:

> Palmer and Crandall (1977) compared murder rates in 10 pairs of
> neighboring states with different capital punishment laws. In 8 of
> the 10 pairs, murder rates were *higher* in the state with capital pun-
> ishment. This research opposed the deterrent effect of the death
> penalty.

After reading the cards, the students were asked to rate, on a
16-point scale, how much their attitudes had been swayed by the
card (if at all). Following this, the students were given further materials to read. Some of the materials criticized the conclusions on the
card, even stating that the studies from which the conclusion had
been drawn were now discredited. Once again, the students were
asked how to rate how the additional information affected their
point of view.

A number of surprising conclusions emerged from the study.
First, it found that the students who held positions *against* capital
punishment were not at all swayed by new studies that supported
its use. Likewise, students who were *for* capital punishment were
not swayed by new studies that argued against it. In other words,
the students clung to their previous beliefs: If data supported that
position, they embraced the data. If the evidence didn't support the
position, they ignored it. But the more worrisome discovery was
that when a student had accepted a position, and found evidence
to support that position—and then was told that that information was erroneous or discredited—the student didn't discard the
flawed information. Instead, he or she used it anyway, regardless of
its paucity, to support the original point of view.

"Their sin," noted the researchers, "lay in their readiness to
use evidence already processed in a biased manner to bolster the
very theory or belief that initially justified the processes bias." In

other words, new information is not likely to bring badly polarized groups together, but is merely fuel for their fire of dissension.

Here's another study that takes that thought even further: At the height of the presidential race of 2004, a group of participants—15 of them committed Democrats and 15 committed Republicans— agreed to literally have their heads examined. In this case, research- ers put the participants into fMRI machines, where they were asked to read statements that insulted the credibility of their candidates.[25]

So, in the case of John Kerry:

Initial statement: During the 1996 campaign, Kerry told a *Boston Globe* reporter that the Social Security system should be over- hauled. He said Congress should consider raising the retirement age and means-testing benefits. "I know it's going to be unpopu- lar," he said. "But we have a generational responsibility to fix this problem."

Contradictory statement: This year, on *Meet the Press,* Kerry pledged that he will never tax or cut benefits to seniors or raise the age for eligibility for Social Security.

Exculpatory statement: Economic experts now suggest that, in fact, the Social Security system will run out of money in 2049, not 2020 as they had thought in 1996.

How would Kerry supporters react to this apparently damag- ing statement? Would they rationally accept the criticism—which would show up as activity in the cool-thinking cerebral area of the brain? Or would they fight it, with an explosion of activity in the emotionally charged amygdala. As you may have suspected (from your own experience with the TV pundits), the researchers found that Kerry supporters' amygdalae exploded in indignation. The prefrontal cortex, meanwhile, home of cool reasoning, showed very little activity. The researchers saw one thing overwhelmingly: a rush to an emotional defense.

To be fair and balanced, let's step inside the heads of some George Bush supporters. I'll try to interpret the evidence, so that we see what happens when their man tells what seems to be a whopper:

Initial statement: "First of all, Ken Lay is a supporter of mine. I love the man. I got to know Ken Lay years ago, and he has given generously to my campaign. When I'm president, I plan to run the country like a CEO runs a country. Ken Lay and Enron are a model for how I'll do that."

fMRI reaction: Sensing an ambush, the amygdala flashes alarm, sparks brightly, and then fades quickly. With that one spark, however, it has sent notice to the rest of the brain to prepare to fight—or flee.

Contradictory statement: Mr. Bush now avoids any mention of Ken Lay and is critical of Enron when asked.

fMRI reaction: Now we see activity in the left lateral inferior frontal cortex and left insula, both consistent with the processing of negative information. The lights are sparking as well in the inferior orbital frontal cortex, where emotions are processed, and the precuneus, which is known to handle evaluative judgments.

Exculpatory statement: People who know the president report that he feels betrayed by Ken Lay, and was genuinely shocked to find that Enron's leadership had been corrupt.

Reaction: Okay, we've got activity in the medial prefrontal cortex, including a large area of activation that includes the ventral subdivision of the anterior cingulate, extending into the ventromedial prefrontal cortex—a region associated with the processing of emotional influences on reasoning. Finally, the ventral stratum lights up: This reflects apparent relief with having resolved the nettlesome issue—quite possibly celebrated with a nip of dopamine.

The study concluded that Kerry supporters reacted just as emotionally to attacks on their man as did the Bush supporters. In both cases, the confirmation bias was alive and well—and keeping all the participants well sealed in the lockbox of irrational reasoning.

The emotional brain, then, keeps all of us in lockboxes. It comprises one of the greatest challenges to visionaries: to get outside the walls, to rise over the yes-men and sycophants and even their confidence in their own ideas, to be able to see clearly.

What happens when we all are in lockboxes? A great example of the consequences has been created by physicists Lada Adamic and Natalie Glance.[26] During the 2004 presidential election, Adamic and Glance charted the connections between hundreds of blogs. One might suppose that the Internet would give people the opportunity to hear a variety of views—that people's minds would be enlarged through the spirited cacophony of many opinions. But Adamic and Glance found that, on the Internet, at least, we are all talking to ourselves—or at least to those who will support and feed supportive evidence to our cherished beliefs.

The figure shown on the next page depicts what they found, with liberal bloggers on the left and the conservatives on the right. As you can see, both groups are preaching to the choir—with very few lines of communication between them.

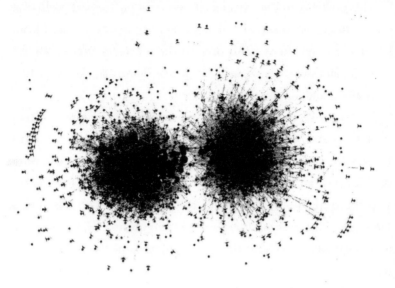

In the same way, we often are left preaching to ourselves: We see what we expect to see. We believe what confirms our expectations—what supports our beliefs. We are confident about our opinions, even cocky. Alarmingly, we are willing to knowingly use flawed data, as long as they support the position we want to keep alive.

That's the confirmation bias—the hardwired lockbox that visionaries must either break out of or succumb to. No wonder so few of us can break through these walls of deception and actually see the world as it is!

For all the mistakes that visionaries can make, there is one gaffe that is made most often by boards of directors and others charged with keeping companies alive and vibrant. This is the hiring of a visionary from one company or institution into their own— usually at quite an expense on the front end, and even more on the back.

The problem is that visionaries don't often transfer well from one domain to another. If you can imagine putting Richard Branson into a gray suit at IBM, or even the likes of a Warren Buffett onto the Branson houseboat, well, it just doesn't work. Yet it happens again and again.

Look at Robert Nardelli, the former CEO of The Home Depot. A star at GE, Nardelli was certainly viewed as a visionary when he was hired by the home improvement retailer. Indeed, he did double revenues for a while, until a slowing economy put the bite into the business. But it was Nardelli's poor fit with The Home Depot's culture that was the rub: Nardelli pushed GE's beloved Six Sigma quality control strategy into every corner of the company, made massive cuts in personnel, and came across as arrogant and uncaring. Worse, he insisted on big bonuses even when the stock was plummeting. Once a visionary, he was, in the words of *Business-Week,* a "flameout."

Or take Richard Thomas. Thomas was a star at IBM under Lou Gerstner. But when he joined Xerox he infuriated the sales force by divvying up their accounts by industry (rather than by territory) and offended R&D by forcing them to spend more time on Six Sigma exercises than they had for actual research. The biggest gaffe of all was Thomas's suggestion that Xerox PARC, the research center that had invented the mouse and the graphical user interface (and that was as central to Xerox's corporate identity as the Magic Kingdom is to Disney), be axed. Thomas lasted three years before being shown the door. Sure, he was once a star, but when he got to Xerox, his star imploded.

Jim McNerney, the former CEO of 3M, is another fallen visionary. Once a contender for Jack Welch's job at GE, McNerney went to 3M, and with Welch's hard-knuckled approach, fired 11 percent of the workforce (8,000 employees) and once again brought in Six Sigma. Profits rose dramatically but McNerney was accused of killing the innovative heartbeat of the company, and was shown the door.

The march of "visionary" CEOs off the cliff is, in fact, almost an ordinary occurrence: You have Pat Russo at Alcatel-Lucent, who, in that particular Anglo-French merger, failed to recognize the different vibes of a French company. You have Paul Pressler, a star at Walt Disney, who hobbled the free-wheeling Gap Inc. culture with a labyrinthine bureaucracy, alienated its designers, and was finally fired. The list goes on and on.

But perhaps the most memorable visionary flameout was John Sculley, whose tenure at Apple ended in 1993. Sculley was the president of PepsiCo before joining Steve Jobs at Apple in 1983. Jobs thought that Sculley was a real catch, and he was. Sculley joined Pepsi in 1967 and soon proved himself an "impatient perfectionist," in his own words, someone who challenged the company's conventional wisdom. In a business where one point of market share translates itself into $100 million in sales, Sculley was a marketing wizard, who intuitively knew how to throw Pepsi's weight around to its best advantage.

Sculley's claim to fame was the Pepsi Challenge, the marketing coup that he championed, and which eventually allowed Pepsi to unseat Coke as America's number one soft drink (Sculley admits that he took the Pepsi Challenge once and, oops, chose Coke. Fortunately the media wasn't around to notice his gaffe).[27] So Sculley was a certified visionary. But then he joined Apple.

At first Sculley and Jobs were Apple's dynamic duo. But that didn't last long. Their relationship soon soured, and eventually took on Machiavellian proportions when Sculley had Jobs fired. The fates apparently didn't like that, for once Jobs was gone, Sculley began to fail as well. Sculley's fall from grace has been variously blamed on Sculley's inflation of the price of the Mac, which pushed customers to the IBM PC; or his failed attempt to personally steer the engineering of Apple products. But in the end it was vision more than anything else that Sculley lacked. He just didn't have Jobs's foresight. The company had lost its leader, and its direction. In 1993, Sculley was pushed out.

But Sculley wasn't the only former visionary to fail at Apple. Gil Amelio, Apple's next CEO (after a short stint by Michael Spindler, who left after his doctor warned him the stress might be fatal), failed as well. Amelio rode into Apple on a big horse: he had a PhD in physics and a best-selling book, *Profit from Experience*. Moreover, he had a sterling track record, having taken National Semiconductor, as CEO, from staggering losses in 1993 to record-breaking profitability in 1996.

When Amelio became CEO, most people wanted Apple, which was sliding into bankruptcy, to be sold for scrap. Not Amelio; he thought Apple could be saved.

That's vision for you, but in Amelio's case, failure loomed. As it turned out, he had neither the consumer marketing experience to save Apple, nor the charisma that Apple's product development wizards required. In Amelio's first year, Apple lost another billion dollars, and by the next, Amelio was out.

In his tell-all memoir, *On the Firing Line: My 500 Days at Apple,* Amelio groused about the size of his severance package and noted, "If I had stayed at National Semiconductor, beyond not having had my reputation tarnished, I would have continued to accumulate wealth at roughly $5 million a year and would have clearly been ahead."[28] Such is the bitter taste of failed vision.

Oddly, Steve Jobs was setting himself up for a similar situation at at Pixar. Jobs was a brilliant visionary. But he was making the mistake of seeing everything in terms of computers. He still didn't see that the real value of the company lay in the great things that

Lasseter, Catmull, and the others were doing there with computer animation.

Of course, Jobs's vision may have been clouded by Pixar's financial distress. It was losing about $10 million a year. As a result, relates Alan Deutschman in *The Second Coming of Steve Jobs,* Jobs decided in 1990 that he had no choice but to sell Pixar's proprietary piece of hardware—the Pixar Image Computer. In its place, Pixar would refocus on the TV commercials it had just started making (for the likes of Listerine and Life Savers candy) and two pieces of software, RenderMan and IceMan. Jobs didn't close down Pixar's little animation unit, although he came very close.

You could fade this scene to black, but then something miraculous happened: Pixar's little animation films began to get noticed. It started with Lasseter's animation short about the father and son Luxo lamps—the expressive, anthropomorphic lamps that appear at the beginning of most Pixar films. Then came *Red's Dream,* about a forlorn little unicycle. *Tin Toy* was next, and pleased even Jobs when it won the 1988 Academy Award for best short animated film.

Pixar's fledgling success even attracted Disney's attention: When the Disney people found that Pixar's software and techniques could digitally ink and paint animation cells, replacing the former costly, time-intensive process of hand painting each animation cell, they decided to test the company on some of the cells being made for *The Little Mermaid.* That worked out so well that they gave Pixar the complete job for their next feature, *Rescuers Down Under.* More important, as David A. Price relates in *The Pixar Touch,* Jeffrey Katzenberg, Disney's animation chief, began to talk with Lasseter and Catmull about a full-length feature. After tough negotiations in July 1991 (Jobs didn't get the price he wanted, but won a three-picture deal instead), they signed a contract to start work on a feature that would be called *Toy Story.*

The project went through several ups and downs, and was almost canceled in November 1993 by Disney over script concerns. But by March 1994, with a new script, it was back on track. For each week of work by Pixar's group of 124 animators (and 117 Sun Microsystems computers), *Toy Story* gained three minutes of animation.[29]

You are probably thinking that by now Jobs *finally* recognized the real value of Pixar, and was clapping his hands in delight. But neither is true. Rather, Jobs was deeply concerned: In just five years he had sunk nearly $55 million into Pixar and now—under the astringent terms of the contract Pixar had signed with Disney—was liable for millions more in overruns. Meanwhile, Jobs's NeXT computer company was in danger as well. By some accounts, Jobs had $25 million to go before he was broke. So even while work progressed on *Toy Story,* one could understand why Jobs was out—again—trying to sell the Pixar *computer* to anyone he could. Once again, some of the former suitors gathered around, from Hallmark to Siemens to GE.

Finally, Microsoft stepped forward. A deal to buy Pixar was agreed upon. The date was set to sign. And then—in a scene that might have come from *Toy Story* itself—Jobs's eyes suddenly snapped open to the opportunity before him. The epiphany happened like this: In January 1995 Disney had scheduled a press briefing for *Toy Story.* It was being held in New York's Central Park, under a huge tent with a 100-seat theater inside. Michael Eisner, then-mayor Rudy Giuliani, and even Roy Disney Jr. were there. "That Disney had been able to stage the briefing in the middle of Central Park was amazing enough," explains David Price in *The Pixar Touch.* "What Jobs heard about the *Pocahontas* premiere impressed him even more: Disney had persuaded the city to let it take over the Great Lawn in Central Park in early June, fence it off, and put up seven-story-high cinema screens. Up to a hundred thousand people would be invited. The panache and extravagance of the event seemed amazing."

"*That* was the moment when Steve realized the Disney deal would materialize into something much bigger than he had ever imagined," *Toy Story* producer Ralph Guggenheim told writer Alan Deutschman.[30] Finally, Jobs could appreciate the dream that Catmull and Smith had carried with them for the better part of a decade: computer-animated *features*.

Stepping back from his earlier decisions, Jobs abruptly informed Microsoft he would only *license* to them some of Pixar's patents for a one-time fee of $6.5 million. "Steve kind of jerked back," Pam Kerwin, Pixar's VP of marketing at the time, told Price, "because, I think, there was something visceral in him that said, 'This is really going to be stupendous.'"[31] And indeed it was.

But now Jobs was on to an even bigger vision. It went beyond the gathering conviction that *Toy Story* would be a big hit: Jobs had decided that once the film was officially released on November 22, 1995, he would take Pixar public. It was an outrageous idea, since Pixar was $55 million in the hole and had never ever made a profit. But Netscape had just had a fabulous IPO after merely a year in business. And so Pixar could do it as well.

And that's why, as Brent Schlender and I waited for him at the curb of his childhood home, Jobs was on his car phone, furiously working the deal.

Toy Story was released on November 22 and became an instant smash. The Pixar IPO was set for November 29. When the markets opened that morning, Pixar started at $22. At one point it hit a high of nearly $50, and ended in the afternoon at $39. All together, the offering raised nearly $140 million, the largest IPO of the year for any company.

Jobs, with 80 percent of the firm, saw his shares rising in value to more than $1.1 billion. Notes David Price, "The *rounding error* on that figure was almost as much as the entire value of his Apple holdings when he left Apple a decade earlier."[32]

That's vision. Or luck. Or intuition. Or all three rolled up into one. Whatever it was, Jobs had hit his nadir in November 1993, and by the end of 1995, he was back on top once again.

CHAPTER NINE

When Genius Fails

"No one in particular is a good predictor of anything. Sorry."

—Nassim Nicholas Taleb, *The Black Swan*

It was quite a party at the house of scientist Stuart Kauffman. His sprawling, modern abode looked out at the mountains and the rugged, rocky terrain of New Mexico. The wine and food were abundant, the conversation animated, and in the end Kauffman even sat down at his drum set and banged out a few tunes.

Sixty years ago scientists of his caliber might have been at the Manhattan Project nearby, building the bomb that would eventually end World War II and begin the nuclear age. That was a challenge in itself, of course. But now Kauffman and his fellow scientists at the Santa Fe Institute faced a different problem. While their studies into complexity theory were intriguing—and while the scientists continued to invite military brass and corporate leaders to lunch to discuss it—the problem was that, unlike several scientific pursuits enjoying the dot-com boom, it wasn't generating much cash.

There was hope that complexity theory might create some kind of new business tool—after all, the theory helps one model the components of almost any system, including businesses or even entire industries. The problem, the scientists found, was that business people didn't want to know what *had* happened—they wanted to know what *will* happen. I sat through one presentation in which a scientist sliced apart the oil industry, revealing the complex interaction among its parts. But at the end the oil men wanted to know what this meant for the future, say, a few years out. In all candor, the scientist replied wistfully, it meant very little.[1]

At least the complexity wizards were being honest.

When we think of visionaries, we think of someone whose gaze into the future goes far beyond our own. How else could they make those great bets, time and again, that lead them out of obscurity and onto the front pages of *Fortune* and *Time*?

But besides the true visionaries, there's a whole pack of faux visionaries out there, urging us to believe that they can actually see the future. These *visionaries prix fixe*—who profit from pretending to peer into the future—are far more willing to tout the prescience of their wares than reveal their shortcomings.

The media is packed with experts who see six hurricanes bearing down on the coast in a season, or stocks moving up 10 percent to a particular level of success, or one country invading another on a certain date. The pundits, the talking heads, the columnists: These people *are visionaries,* we are reminded time and again. When we see them on TV, they certainly seem to be comfortable with the title, and the salary, no matter how wrong their predictions turn out to be.

The media pundits are just the beginning. We also have federal prognosticators like the National Weather Service, the Federal Reserve, the Council of Economic Advisers. We have the financial services industry gurus (represented by the mutual fund companies, stock brokerage firms, investment research firms). We have the global thinkers, like the World Bank. And then there are the think tanks, advocacy groups, university forecasting services, consulting firms, private weather forecasting firms, life insurers, political columnists, the CIA—all churning out forecasts. In America alone, as William Sherden notes in *The Fortune Sellers,* forecasting is a multibillion-dollar business, employing hundreds of thousands of people.[2]

The underlying irony of the forecasting business, however, is that no one can *really* call the really long shots. No one.

Countless studies have quantified this. In one, the S&P index predictions of several distinguished economists were tracked from 1952 to 1986. The conclusion? The economists were found to have had "no predictive powers."[3]

In another study, this by the Harvard Institute of Economic Research, researchers reviewed the prognostications of 153 stock advice newsletters. The conclusion? The tip sheets showed "no significant evidence of stock picking ability."[4]

Between 1984 and 1999, another study concluded, almost 90 percent of all mutual fund managers had underperformed the Wilshire 5000 Index.[5]

In still another study, this of 48 predictions made by economists, 46 of them missed significant turning points in the economy. Overall, the forecasts were about as accurate as flipping coins, the study concluded. But there were a few exceptions: The forecasts of the Federal Reserve, the Council of Economic Advisers, and the Congressional Budget Office were actually worse than pure chance.[6]

Political pundits are no more successful. One study spanning two decades tracked the predictions of 280 "experts," who eventually arrived at 82,361 forecasts. The results were not favorable for the *visionaries prix fixe:* Their forecasts were poorer than you could have made by flipping a coin. Not only that, the so-called specialists in any field made worse predictions than the generalists. In fact, the more *prominent* the forecaster, the more frequently he or she proved to be *wrong*.[7]

It goes on and on—from sublimity to hilarity: In 1984 *The Economist* magazine asked four ex-finance ministers, four students at Oxford University, four chairmen of multinational firms, and four London trash collectors to make regular economic forecasts. Ten years later the magazine revealed the results. Guess whose predictions were best? As it turned out, the four multinational corporate chairmen won—but joining them at the top of the heap (in a tie) were the trash collectors.[8]

Even the *Wall Street Journal*'s famous "dart tossing" contest suggested faint praise for the forecasting skills of the *visionaries prix fixe*. It began when economist Burton Malkiel remarked in *A Random Walk Down Wall Street* that "a blindfolded monkey throwing darts at a newspaper's financial pages could select a portfolio that would do just as well as one carefully suggested by experts."[9]

The *Wall Street Journal* took up the challenge in 1988, substituting the monkey for the next best thing (in the eyes of its editors): *Wall Street Journal* reporters tossing darts at stock tables posted on the wall. The dart throwing continued for 14 years, with investment experts picking stocks based on analysis and the reporters throwing darts. In the end, said the *Journal,* the managed stocks averaged 10.2 percent versus 3.5 percent for the darts. But an argument broke out about how you sliced and diced the data. One study showed that the stock pickers won 61 of 100 contests. That might be considered good, the study noted, but losing 39 percent of the time to four darts is nothing to brag about.[10]

Even that victory was dimmed, argued Malkiel: Since the investment pros named their stocks at the beginning of each contest cycle, the stocks they named enjoyed a "publicity effect" and abnormal gains for several days to come. Without that artificial advantage, Malkiel maintained, they would have likely done worse than the darts. The *Journal,* not willing to get sucked into any more monkey business, ended the fray in 2002 by asserting it "isn't declaring a winner."

A lack of prescience when it comes to picking stocks, of course, is small change compared to bigger forecasting errors. For starters, you could pick the 2008 economic collapse, which most economists and *visionaries prix fixe*—despite their "elegant" and "disciplined" econometric models—missed or failed to call.

So, what does that say for the multibillion-dollar forecasting industry? Most of the critics don't blunt their words. Says Nassim Nicholas Taleb in *The Black Swan:* "I find it scandalous that in spite of the empirical record, we continue to project into the future as if we were good at it . . . We are suckers for those who help us navigate uncertainty, whether the fortune teller or the well-published academics, or civil servants using phony science."[11]

Says William Sherden, an adjunct professor at the Brandeis University International Business School and author of *The Fortune Sellers,* "Our belief in these everyday prophecies is the adult version of the childhood belief in the Tooth Fairy or the Easter Bunny."[12]

One could also quote from Nobel Prize–winning economist Merton Miller: "It's a game, it's a chance operation," he has said of stock picking. "People think they are doing something purposeful, but they're really not."[13]

So with the abysmal record of the forecasters—no better than a flip of the coin or the toss of a dart in most cases—why do we insist on listening to them? Why do we pay piles of cash to the faux visionaries when we *know* that they are emperors without any clothes?

The overwhelming reason is that the brain abhors confusion. It doesn't like ambiguity or randomness. It has a deep-rooted need for order. What we want is *control* over our environments, and wherever we can find it—even from questionable sources—we'll take it. Even if we know it's probably wrong.

What's remarkable is that, in the absence of a real pattern, we will simply make one up. In one study participants were asked to press the space bar on a keyboard in order to make a green dot appear on a screen. They actually had no control over the dot at all, which appeared randomly. But they *thought* they had found the key to the pattern regardless. (The participant who first watched a video about an unjust, inefficient government reported better control of the screen than those who didn't watch the video—a result that suggests that people who feel out of control tend to believe that they can compensate through more control of their own.)[14]

Another study asked professional traders to use a computer mouse to control a dot on a screen. The traders felt that they had some control over the situation—even though the mouse was not even connected to the computer. Other experiments asked people to find the images in snowy video screens. They inevitably "found" some—although no images existed.[15]

Once again, the more the subjects were prompted to feel that they were *out of control* (for instance, by reading that financial markets are volatile or that government is unjust and inefficient or even that the weather is unpredictable), the *more* patterns they saw in what were random events.

We want control over the random aspects of life. It is why, researchers find, that when playing craps, people tend to throw the dice harder for high numbers and softer for low numbers: We want to feel that we can actually nudge randomness onto our side.

It all goes back to that struggle between the anxious amygdala and the pensive prefrontal cortex: While our rational minds realize that we can't really influence the dice by tossing them harder, our emotional mind insists it might be worthwhile. That's why we can't resist the talking heads on TV.

In this complex and arguably dangerous world, we want as much long-term forecasting as we can obtain. We ache to know the future. And that's what *visionaries prix fixe* sell—our insecurity about approaching storms, financial booms and busts, social calamities, and all the rest. "No matter how much evidence exists that seers do not exist," Wharton professor J. Scott Armstrong wrote in *Technology Review,* "suckers will pay for the existence of seers." By the way, this is what he calls his "Seersucker Theory."[16]

What is it exactly that the *visionaries prix fixe* see that they can peddle to the rest of us? Actually, they are pandering to a quirk of nature, a trick played on humans in particular, since we are inveterate pattern hunters.

Some years ago a mathematician decided to design a brick wall for the inside of her home. The wall would have red, white, and black bricks, and she decided, being a mathematician, that she would cleverly use a mathematical table to distribute the bricks randomly.

The problem was that when she got through with her design, the bricks in the wall didn't *look* random. In fact, one area had nothing but black bricks. In the end, she had to design the wall by eye—moving the bricks around so that they didn't seem to fall into any particular pattern.[17]

So what's going on here? This example reveals a surprising idea: Randomness is not as *random looking* as we think it is. "Random distribution," in fact, is not even or evenly distributed. It's streaky, clumpy. That comes as a big surprise to most of us. Isn't random suppose to mean evenly dispersed?[18]

Let me give you another example: the random shuffle feature of an Apple iPod.

In a recent post on the tech review Web site CNET.com, one iPod user complained that while using the "random setting on her [iPod], the songs still seemed to be falling into patterns . . . I had a playlist of 50 songs on shuffle . . . There was one song that was in the playback list twice and surprise, surprise, Apple's 'shuffle' feature played them back to back!"[19]

Said another, "I've noticed this too. Whenever I randomize my playlists the same artists are played: Taylor Swift, Cobra Starship, Flo-Rida, Kanye West, and Pink and other artists that are famous right now."

Said a third, "For those of you who use your iPod heavily, you've probably noticed that your supposedly random 'shuffling' iPod seems to be particularly fond of the Bee Gees, Melissa Etheridge, and Pavarotti."

What's going on? Some of the chat on the blog turned to conspiracy theories. Perhaps certain record labels were *paying* Apple a fee to make their songs appear more frequently? Could it be? Then another theory appeared: Perhaps Apple is *monitoring* our use—and to please us, secretly juicing up the selection based on the song that we play most often. Could it be?

Newsweek correspondent Steven Levy picked up on the controversy and contacted Apple. Before long, he found himself posing the question to Steve Jobs himself. Jobs, in turn, got on the phone and consulted one of Apple's engineers. The engineer assured Steve that the shuffle feature was indeed random—the algorithm that does the shuffling had been tested and verified.

That seemed to satisfy Levy, until he got an iPod Shuffle himself, which has a feature called autofill, loading the player with a supposedly random selection of 120 or so songs from his much larger overall collection—in his case, more than 3,000 tunes. What bothered Levy was that there were several disturbing clusters, including three tracks from the same album.

That sent Levy over to the office of Temple University professor John Allen Paulos, an expert in mathematical theory. Paulos explained that it's quite possible to see runs like six head tosses of a coin in a row. (In a series of 20 coin tosses, in fact, you have a 10 percent chance of getting a streak of 6 of the same side in a row, a 25 percent chance of 5 in a row, and a 50-50 chance of getting 4 heads in a row.)[20]

In the long run, however, the odds will even out. But in the meantime, our brains feel that they have found a pattern. It isn't true, but it sure seems convincing. That's why bloggers saw a "pattern" on their iPods and immediately began to wonder why.

The fact that randomness is streaky might cause someone some problems designing a wall for your home, or elicit some complaints over the performance of one's iPod, but it causes bigger problems when we mistake random streaking for meaningful patterns.

One example that has been widely cited is the dispersion of German "buzz bombs" that fell on London during the Blitz in World War II. There was nothing more random than the landing of the bombs, which were sent across the channel via spluttery V-1 and V-2 rockets. In most cases, when the fuel ran out, or when a line was intentionally cut by a crude timing mechanism, the rocket nosed downward into the city.

What was significant at the time was that the bombs seemed to fall mostly on the working-class East Enders. That in turn had the newspapers creating theories that the Germans were intentionally beating up on the working class in order to alienate London's poor from the rich. Or that the German V-2's guidance system was better than was supposed. Or even that German spies must reside in the areas that were less frequently hit.

As it turned out, an analysis after the war found the hits to be random. But it was a streaky random distribution—a meaningless pattern, in fact—that still set rumors spreading.[21]

As you can see, randomness can create pseudopatterns, which the brain then spins into stories. And they can be quite convincing. It happened with the Apple iPod and with the German buzz bombs, and it happens whenever financial information, social topics, the weather, or any other issue lands on the plate of forecasters.

For the experts in probability, then, streakiness is what forecasters generally stumble upon and sell as prescience. You have a mutual fund with three successive years of success? Or a stock picker who is rated by the financial magazines as the best there is? Or even a Sunday morning TV pundit who predicts foreign affairs better than the crowd? All of them are suggesting a meaningful pattern in what is merely the "streakiness" of chance.

As a result, a string of good or bad quarters need not have any "cause" at all. In fact, randomness expert Leonard Mlodinow argues in *The Drunkard's Walk* that many seemingly "extraordinary" events—from the hot streaks of athletes to an extraordinary run of corporate profits—are not really meaningful patterns at all, but random streaks. "When we look at extraordinary accomplishments in sports—or elsewhere—we should keep in mind that extraordinary events can happen without extraordinary causes," he says.[22]

But that doesn't prevent the *visionaries prix fixe* from jumping on them and spinning convincing stories to make us think they are true. In fact, Mlodinow mentions one stock picker who really was extraordinarily accurate—correctly predicting the market for some 19 years. Did this guy have some sort of special insight? Not at all. He was a columnist for the *Sporting News,* and his "method" pivoted on the Super Bowl (NFL win, stock market up; AFL win, market down). "Had he had different credentials—and not revealed his method—he could have been hailed as the most clever analyst since Charles H. Dow," said Mlodinow.[23]

To be fair, *visionaries prix fixe* can be as misled by random streaks as the rest of us. In fact, they are sometimes more blind, because after a few chance wins they become convinced that their superior knowledge, or even their popularity on TV, has given them the special touch. Of course, they're dead wrong.

University of California at Berkeley professor Philip Tetlock says that when experts know too much they begin to construct "compelling cause-effect scenarios." These scenarios are very detailed and quite seductive, but unfortunately, they generally add up to what Dr. Tetlock calls "a hot air hypothesis."[24] The big surprise in this, of course, is that people who know *less* about something often know *more* about it than the "experts"—at least in terms of seeing the bigger picture. Maybe this shouldn't come as such a surprise: It was the little boy, after all, who saw that the emperor wore no clothes.

But there's more to the work of *visionaries prix fixe* than that. After they see the patterns, the next step is to create the story that binds them together. And in this, the brain also makes some egregious mistakes. Let me give an example.

Shortly after 11:30 on the morning of January 28, 1986, the space shuttle *Challenger* exploded. The following morning, Emory University psychology professors Ulric Neisser and Nicole Harsch handed out a questionnaire to 106 Psychology 101 students. Among the questions asked were: How did you first hear about the *Challenger* explosion? Where were you? What were you doing? Who were you with? What time of day was it? How did you feel?

The questionnaires were left untouched for nearly two and a half years. Then, in the fall of 1988, the researchers went searching for the original subjects. They found 44 of them and repeated the questions they had asked 30 months earlier. Surprisingly only 25 percent of the students even remembered filling out the earlier questionnaire. Beyond that, their recollections of where they were and what they were doing when the *Challenger* exploded were far different from their first recollections.

One student had originally recalled that he was returning to his dorm with a friend when he ran into another friend (from Switzerland) who urged him to turn on the TV. "Why?" he replied. "Just turn it on!" his friend exclaimed. So he and his other friend bounded up the stairs. His friend thought it might be about a war in the Middle East. He thought it might be a presidential assassination. They burst into the room and turned on the TV. Another friend joined them. "What time was this?" the researchers asked. "1:10," he replied. "What were you doing previously?" "I was trying to start my car." "Who was with you when you learned about the explosion?" "My friend, who was in the room with me."

Two and half years later, the student's remembrance had changed. Now he said that he was merely walking through the hall of his dorm when he heard a commotion. "Somebody must have told me what happened," he told the researchers, adding that he then went to his room and turned on the TV. "What time was this?" the researchers asked. "11:30." "What were you doing previously?" "Just returning to my dorm room." "Who was with you when you learned about the explosion?" "No one. I was alone."

An experienced trial lawyer might just smile at this, knowing how eyewitness testimony is often wildly unreliable, but it came as a surprise to the researchers. The results confirmed that memory is a slippery thing: Of the 44 students, 25 percent were wrong in their remembrance about *everything* and scored zero. Fifty percent were right on one major point and wrong about two others. Only 7 percent, or three of the students, were right on all counts, and even then they had some minor discrepancies in their recall.

The big surprise, however, was how confident the students were in the accuracy of their recall: Of the 20 students who were *most* confident that their memories were correct, several were *completely wrong* and others were *largely wrong* in their recall.

Even when the researchers tried to prompt the right recollections from the students, they didn't change their minds or reshape their answers to conform to what they had originally said. In fact—and perhaps most surprising of all—when the students were shown their original statements, most of them couldn't recognize them as their own!

"No one who had given an incorrect account in the original interview even pretended that they now recalled what was stated on the original record," the researchers noted. "On the contrary they kept saying, 'As I told you, I have no recollection of that at all,' or, 'I still think it's the other way around.'" Finally, they noted, "As far as we can tell, the original memories are just gone."[25]

In 1961, a group of thirteen- and fourteen-year-old boys living near Chicago made a poor choice: They impulsively pulled a fire alarm. Within minutes, the police and fire departments arrived. The kids, watching, then made their second bad choice: When two officers jumped out of their cruiser (leaving the motor running), the kids jumped in. They drove the car around the streets of Chicago with the lights flashing and sirens wailing.

When the cruiser ran out of gas, the kids tumbled out, returned by bus, and turned themselves in. The police, thoroughly embarrassed, didn't press charges (the early 1960s were kindler and gentler times). But the community, shocked, wanted some answers: What was wrong with these kids? Was this just a normal teenage prank—or the sign of a real emotional disturbance in their midst?

The incident inspired Daniel Offer, a Northwestern University psychiatrist, to investigate. By the following year he had set up a study in which he interviewed 73 high school freshmen (from two high schools near Chicago). He asked each of them a series of questions: Did their parents encourage them to be active in sports? Was religion helpful to them? Did they receive physical punishment as discipline? Do they date much? Ever had sex?

Dr. Offer kept up with the kids until they graduated in 1969. The eventual results were reassuring: Seventh and eighth grade, they revealed, was the time that boys generally push away from their parents (mostly over issues like making their beds, how to dress, and who their friends would be). It can even get a bit wild: turning over garbage cans, vandalism, physical fights, even stealing a car.

But in the case of Dr. Offer's group, most of the kids didn't go wild, and even those who did, noted the study, "committed only one delinquent act and then abandoned this form of behavior." By the tenth grade almost all of the boys had settled down and shifted their focus elsewhere: By the end of their freshmen year, 45 percent of the boys had been on a date. By their junior year, 30 percent had experienced heavy petting. Ten percent had had sex.

The study is interesting, but what makes it unique is that in 1996 (34 years later), Dr. Offer was able to round up most of the group—now age forty-eight—once again. What he found was fascinating—if only because it painted a picture of "Regular Guys" (as Dr. Offer's book is titled).

The stars of the class came out well (as expected). But so did the nerds. In fact, in telling their stories, both the stars and nerds described running the same gauntlet of life's challenges—from divorces and bad career choices to illnesses and drug use—to emerge, by midlife, pretty content (the study seems to confirm that adversity generally makes people better). Even in their adult vices—22 percent were obese, 7 percent smoked marijuana, 15 percent consumed three or more drinks a day—they were right on the mark in terms of national averages in the USA.

But for our purposes, what was amazing about the 1996 study was how little of the detail of their teen years the participants remembered correctly. For instance, while 60 percent had recalled parental encouragement to be active in sports in the 1960s, fewer than 40 percent remembered it years later. In the 1960s nearly

70 percent had said that religion was helpful; by the 1990s less than 25 percent remembered it being so. And while 90 percent recalled being physically punished by their parents as kids (in the 1960s survey), by 1996 only a third recalled it being so.

Their memories were a little sharper when it came to their love lives: 77 percent said it was "easy to get a date" while in high school; reflecting back 34 years later, the response was the same for 65 percent of them. Sexual intercourse was another matter: Back in high school, 15 percent had endorsed sex while they were still high schoolers. In 1996, 44 percent, looking back, said they had believed in the 1960s that having sex was okay. Obviously, they had become more liberal over the years.

The two examples illustrate an important point about human behavior: While our memory is generally accurate, individual memories are often flawed. In fact, as researchers have discovered, even vivid memories can be completely wrong.[26]

So how does a memory form? First something goes into our working memory, that busy place that can barely remember a phone number.[27] From there, if we deem it worthy, it passes over to the basal forebrain, a center deep in the cerebral cortex (which is in charge of arranging the individual images according to "earlier" and "later," so that a meaningful action is reconstructed). Certain neurons are linked by dendrites and the pattern is formed.

But memory is not a hardwired circuit, nor certainly nothing like the memory of a computer. Long-term memory, it turns out, is more like a washing machine, with memories rising and sinking beneath the suds, colors bleeding one into another. Every time we remember something, it is different. We are constantly mixing it around with other memories and with what we know from the outside world.[28]

To see how we do this, take your eyes off this page. Now try to recall the previous paragraph. Studies have shown that once we take our eyes off the page, we almost instantly forget what was written—and instantly begin to fill in the blanks with our own content.[29] One study required the subjects to read a few paragraphs of a story, then add a few paragraphs of elaboration and detail of their own. When the subjects were asked the following day to describe the story, most of them described *what they had added,* not what the original story had said.[30] Every time something arises in our consciousness, in other words, it reaches us tailored in a different way. We can't even summon up a memory that we consider particularly vivid and then a few moments later still conjure it up precisely the same way. Give it a try.

What does that tell you about our worth as witnesses? If you want to see who held up a bank, look at the video replay. If you want to recall a conversation, listen to the tape. But if you do have to depend on your memory, recognize that it will probably be a distorted copy of what really transpired.

But that's not all. Memory is also warped by a wide range of biases and distortions, as though one were looking in a funhouse mirror. Daniel Kahneman, for instance, demonstrated through studies that the way we remember things is by the peak experience and how it all ended. So if we had a great day on vacation and it ended well, all the bad stuff in between is forgotten. The "peak/end" is what we've used to summarize the experience.[31]

We also take what we know now and mix it in with what we knew previously. A Caribbean vacation that ended well might be a treasured memory—until one reads that two tourists were eaten the following week by sharks. Then the memory is changed to the story about how you just missed losing your life. This, called hindsight bias, allows us to inform our previous memories with what we know now.[32]

Another bias is in what we commit to memory in the first place. Unlike Las Vegas, not everything that goes into the brain stays in the brain: Many of our memories disappear rapidly, while the ones we keep are often so embellished over time that the long-term memory has little to do with the original event.[33]

Neuroscientists are just now beginning to realize how important the memory is, not only in framing the present, but also in our ability to forecast the future. In fact, some scientists say that in the greater scheme of human survival, memories exist *only* as a tool to make humans better prognosticators. In other words, nature has not installed memories in us for nostalgia's sake, but for the purpose of survival. They help us stay alive another day in this complex world.

To help demonstrate this, let me ask you two questions. First, if you decided to visit your alma mater next year, what would you do on the first day? The second day? Now here's the second question: If you were to visit the African nation of Burkina Faso next year, what would you do on your first day? Your second?

You can answer the first question, of course, because you have an attic full of college memories that you can project forward into the future. The second question probably comes up blank. You don't have any memories to put to the task.[34]

A similar phenomenon arises in an episode from Oliver Sacks's classic book, *The Man Who Mistook His Wife for a Hat*.[35] Sacks, a psychiatrist and neurologist, has a patient who has lost his ability to inform new experiences through the memory of previous ones. Sacks hands the patient (a former professor of music) a rose, and asks him to identify it:

> "About six inches in length . . . A convoluted red form with a linear green attachment."
>
> "Yes," I said encouragingly, "and what do you think it is, Dr. P?"
>
> "Not easy to say." He seemed perplexed. "It lacks the simple symmetry of the Platonic solids, although it may have a higher

symmetry of its own . . . I think this could be an inflorescence or flower."

"Could be?" I inquired.

"Could be," he confirmed.

"Smell it," I suggested, and he again looked somewhat puzzled, as if I had asked him to smell a higher symmetry. But he complied courteously, and took it to his nose. Now, suddenly, he came to life.

"Beautiful," he exclaimed. "An early rose. What a heavenly smell!"

Does the brain become a kind of time traveler, then, dipping into the past and projecting what it retrieves into the future? New research is showing this is true. Our time-traveling abilities seem to be centered in the hippocampus. Several experiments have shown that patients with damage to the hippocampus are left not only without memory, but with the inability to imagine new experiences as well.

In the first of these experiments, researchers at the University of London asked patients to imagine themselves lying on a tropical beach. The healthy subjects conjured up what you might expect: waves lapping the sand, coconut palms, and rustling breezes. For the patients with hippocampus damage, however, the images were different. One noted that he could see only "the color of the blue sky and the white sand . . ."

"Can you see anything else?" the researcher asked. "No, I'm kind of floating," came the reply.[36]

This strong overlap in brain activity between backward and forward mental time travel has been noted in other experiments, some using PET scans and others using MRIs: When subjects were asked to think about the past, and then ponder the future, the activity was found in the regions of the medial prefrontal cortex, the lateral and medial parietal cortex, and the lateral and medial temporal lobes, including, notably, the hippocampus. Said the researchers,

"The medial frontal lobe system, which has been known as crucial for remembering the past, seems to be playing an adaptive value through its ability to provide details that serve as the building blocks of future event simulation."[37] In other words, a crucial role of the memory is to make information available for the simulation of future events.

Some scientists now believe that if memory were meant strictly for rumination, it would have been placed elsewhere in the brain, self-contained. But since it is right on top of the regions necessary for prediction, the role of memory must be to provide information from the past for the simulation of the future.

And there's the rub, in terms of forecasting the future: Everything we can imagine in the future is based somehow on the past. Yet most of the information we need from the past to extrapolate into the future is blurred and distorted, and really not much use in term of its accuracy at all.

In our personal lives, then, if we try to predict the future—even try to predict how we might feel about something—we have to tread carefully. How many of us, for instance, have gone back to our childhood neighborhoods and, for some odd reason, it doesn't seem the same as we remember? Maybe, in fact, we're a little bit let down? We have told ourselves a story about the past that, in reality, may not have been so.

In the world of *prix fixe* forecasting, it is much the same. At the end of the day, forecasters are storytellers. They provide a framework for a streak of chance, be it the reason the German buzz bombs landed on the working class, or why a particular company has had eight quarters of stellar success. But if the facts they are bringing forward to tell their story are flawed, how good will they be when they extrapolate them even farther into the future? If their memories are clouded, how good can their forecasts possibly be?

We are warned that those who don't study history are doomed to repeat it. But history is bent by the same biases and flaws that we see in our personal thoughts. For instance, we may be warned not to repeat the mistakes of the Vietnam War or the Middle East. But what were the mistakes? And how accurately do they lie across the template of a more contemporary situation?

Or what lessons of the 1990s S&L crisis can be applied to today's precarious financial situation? Is our economic future today tracking along the lines of the early 1970s, with a long, hard recession, or the relatively quick rebound of the crash in the early 1980s?

Part of the problem is that the brain likes brevity, and so we tend to reduce history into one- or two-sentence sound bites. The farther back in history you go, the shorter and more opaque they become. The Revolutionary War was fought to free the colonies. The Civil War was fought because the South was for slavery. The Spanish-American War was fought because the Spanish sank the *Maine.* Vietnam was fought to stop Communist expansion.

In the *New Yorker* magazine several years ago, writer Charles McGrath noted that among the staffers at the magazine's offices there was "the tendency to reduce everyone, and every event, to colorful anecdotes."[38] That's not only true at the *New Yorker;* it's true everywhere.

In fact, remember the famous *New Yorker* cover that showed Manhattan in great detail in the foreground, New Jersey in some detail farther back, and the rest of America in the distance as just a few mountain ranges and the sun setting over the Pacific?[39] That's pretty much was happens to our memory as it fades into the distance as well: The details get fewer and fainter, until they disappear.

There's nothing wrong with extrapolating forward from the past. That is the brain's most marvelous trick; we have survived by anticipating everything from the seasons to which snakes have a venomous bite. Much of our time is spent, in fact, extrapolating forward the trends we've observed in the past.

The problem comes when we try for *the long shot,* presuming that what happened before will happen again. That's where our powers of foresight fail. In meteorological forecasting, for instance, most prognostications are accurate for a day or so (depending on the locale). But in the long run, forecasting doesn't work. Temperature forecasts, for instance, are generally no better a few days out than consulting a chart of annual temperature averages.

But no one pays the big bucks for short-term forecasts. We want streaks, and the better the story they come wrapped in, the better we feel. That's why the world is filled with "experts." It is why Washington is packed with former bureaucrats who go into lobbying and industrial consultancies, where they can tell their inside stories to eager ears.

Not only are memories boiled down to sound bites; we can also turn events into even smaller and more opaque units of information called data.

Humans have lots of problems with data. The human brain doesn't understand numbers very well. Researchers have shown that we can comprehend numbers into the thousands, but then they become meaningless. We don't understand a billion of anything, any more than a dog understands the number 12. But we think we do.

The other problem is that we accept numbers very readily. This is another example of Daniel Kahneman's "availability heuristic." In this case it means that people tend to absorb the data that are around them. Not only that, the more we hear that particular fact, the more we believe *it is true.*

What's really odd is that we may discount a piece of data if we know the source—for instance, anything we read off the tabloid rack at the deli check-out line. But the problem is that we often forget the source, and researchers have found that the more we lose track of the source—where we heard or read it—the more convinced we become that it's true. If we see something in a tabloid that is obviously false, in other words, the false fact may gain credence later as we lose track of the dubious source. In the modern world, of course, the problem is that information is flying fast and free. And in that environment, the source is often obscure or at least quickly forgotten.

We are also remarkably gullible. Experiments have shown that simply repeating a false statement over and over leads people to believe that it is true. Likewise, if we repeatedly think or talk about a past experience, we tend to become increasingly confident that we are recalling it accurately.

For instance, it has been bandied about for some time that the average vocabulary of American children has declined dramatically, from about 25,000 words in 1945 to about 10,000 words today. Since this statistic was initially reported in *Harper's* magazine in 1990, it has appeared in countless newspapers, magazines, and science journals, and has been the ammunition for countless arguments—about the risks of video games, the failure of American schools, or the decline of Western civilization itself.

But is it true? Cecil Adams, the intrepid investigator behind the Web site The Straight Dope (www.straightdope.com), decided a few years ago to look into it. First he went back to the original 1945 study, which reviewed 100,000 student compositions containing 6 million words altogether, 25,265 distinct words identified. Next he went back to the 1984 study used by *Harper's* as a comparison. In that case, the researchers studied 5,000 student compositions comprising 500,000 words. From this came the notorious figure of 10,000 vocabulary words.[40]

The problem, Adams explains, is that since the second study

reviewed 60 percent fewer words (6 million versus 500,000), it makes sense that the number of vocabulary words in the 1984 study would be about half of that in 1945. "Some nameless journalist, not thinking too hard, stuck the two numbers together," noted Adams, "and voila: further proof of society's decline."

What's even more surprising (or perhaps not) is that when the author of the 1984 study tried to set the record straight, he could get no one to listen. By then it had become an urban myth (or factoid), a meme that had spread through the media and the Internet. It was dry powder waiting for anyone to use in an explosive argument.

Nassim Nicholas Taleb calls our reliance on dubious data "reasoning correctly from erroneous premises." And that, he notes, was the philosopher John Locke's "precise definition of a madman."[41]

Indeed, it sometimes feels that way. When we find even a kernel of credibility, we buy in. In the late 1980s the rumor floated around that Bobby McFerrin, the creator of the song "Don't Worry, Be Happy," had committed suicide. Another rumor floating around in the 1990s was that Halloween candies contained razor blades. That wasn't true either (although it became a long-lasting urban myth and to this day parents search their kids' candy bags).

While working for the *Wall Street Journal* in London, I noted that the famous English astronomer Patrick Moore told listeners of his popular BBC radio show that there would be a remarkable alignment between Pluto and Jupiter at exactly 9:47 the following morning. The result would be that listeners—if they jumped into the air—might notice a slight lessening of gravity that would make them feel lighter. Thousands tried it and found out it was true (although it was merely an April Fools' joke).

On another occasion, a British TV anchor warned viewers that a local woman had taught her English Sheepdog to drive, and sure enough, viewers saw the happy canine seated behind the wheel of a convertible speedster, tearing down the road, ears flapping in the wind. The station received indignant phone calls from all corners (and later confessed that it was actually a man in a dog suit). Another TV story had a correspondent wandering through the spaghetti groves of Switzerland, remarking on the bumper crop hanging from the trees . . . Well, you get the picture: The British love April Fools' Day.[42]

Forecasting was always suspect in human hands, but with the advent of computers the practice was supposed to reach new levels of success. That's what the *visionaries prix fixe* would like us to believe. And that is why, if you read the prospectuses and brochures of forecasting firms that use computers, you will always see computer-driven models described as "sturdy" and "disciplined"— a vast improvement over human-powered prediction.

Models that predict events governed by physics, such as those used in engineering a bridge, are common and demonstrably useful. But can a chain of supercomputers crunching piles of data really predict the outcome of human events?

Of course, they can't.

Models have several problems. The first is that modeling anything of great complexity, such as the weather—and even more so, human behavior—is impossibly complex. There are more variables that would need to be accounted for than can be considered (recently a Reading University scientist said that climate prediction would not get much better until supercomputers were a thousand times more powerful than they are today).[43]

More important is that the relationship between variables is never clear. In a linear relationship, the variables increase or decrease at a uniform rate; in a nonlinear relationship of complex situations, one may go up arithmetically, while the other goes down—at an exponential rate.[44]

The bigger problem, however, is that no matter how many algorithms you have running, the mathematical formula still needs *assumptions*. We assume, for instance, that Mrs. Smith will stop buying tuna fish when it reaches three dollars a can (that's what she said in the survey). All the computer crunching in the world won't save us, however, if Mrs. Smith reconsiders when tuna hits that price, and decides to keep buying it.

In a famous cartoon by Sidney Harris, a group of scientists are standing before a board covered with scrawled equations. Right in the middle of the elaborate series of calculations are the simple words "And then a miracle happens."[45] That's the weakness of forecasting models as well. Replace "miracle" with "assumption" and you have described the Achilles' heel in computer forecasting.

Another form of error is more blatant. It is when the data are cooked or tweaked to create the conclusion that the forecaster deems correct. In *Useless Arithmetic: Why Environmental Scientists Can't Predict the Future,* environmental scientists Orrin Pilkey and Linda Pilkey-Jarvis say that these misleading studies range from "advocacy" models—data massaged in order to get a preferred message out—to "optimist" models, "personal view" models, "good cause" models, whose goals are self-fulfilling.[46] That's not only bad science—it's bad ethics as well.

One of the more notorious examples of this, they note, was the EPA's 1992 declaration that secondhand smoke was a class A carcinogen, causing the deaths of 3,000 American nonsmokers each year. The problem, as analysis of that claim proceeded, was not only that the EPA had studied 33 previous investigations and chosen 11 for their report. What attracted the real scorn of skeptics was the fact that the EPA had announced the "3,000" statistic *before* the study had even been completed. When it was completed and fell short, the EPA simply went back and doubled the statistical "margin of error" to bring it up to 3,000.

In 1998 a federal judge declared the EPA study null and void, noting that the data had been cherry-picked, and that the agency was "publicly committed to a conclusion before the research had begun."[47]

Questioning the integrity of the data that goes into computer modeling, as well as the assumptions, is at the center of the controversy over global warming. But it pops up frequently in other issues. Jim O'Malley, a former member of the New England Fisheries Management Council, has battled the Canadian government's computer model for the Grand Banks, for instance. O'Malley says that the government mathematical formulas and algorithms that didn't reflect the real complexities of the sea but merely the opinions and ideologies of its creators. As a result of the computer models, the Canadian government permitted more fishing by giant trawlers than they apparently should have, and now the vast schools of cod, some as long as six feet and weighing 200 pounds, are gone.

"I stress that the problem was not mathematics per se," O'Malley wrote in the International Ocean Institute publication *Ocean Yearbook* in 1998, "but the place of idolatry we have given it. And it is idolatry. Like any priesthood, it has developed its own language, rituals and mystical signs to maintain its status and to keep a befuddled congregation subservient, convinced that criticism is blasphemy." In this battle, there has been no resolution: Advocates of the Grand Banks computer modeling defend their science as flawed but still the best tool available. Fishermen who have lost their livelihoods disagree. But one fact is indisputable: The 110,000 square miles that comprise the Grand Banks have been fished to depletion. And no one knows if they will ever return.[48]

It's not just cod that have suffered from computer models, of course. Consider the computer modeling fiasco of Long Term Capital Management, the hedge fund company that Roger Lowenstein described so well in his stunning best seller *When Genius Failed*. The entire $100 billion fund rested on a model of financial markets created by economists Myron Scholes and Robert C. Merton as well as Fischer Black. It rested, as Lowenstein tells us, on the assumption that the volatility of a security is a constant, and therefore market prices would move in "continuous time," or in other words without jagged drops.

That, it turned out, was LTCM's flaw: When the markets in Russia, Eastern Europe, and parts of Latin America collapsed in the summer of 1998, irrationally and suddenly, LTCM's precious model was proven wrong. LTCM was "too big to fail," and was saved only by an infusion of cash from Alan Greenspan and the Fed.

In *The Black Swan* Nassim Nicholas Taleb sums up the life and death of LTCM with his usual piquancy: It was an adventure, he says, "which used the methods and risk expertise of two Nobel economists who were called 'geniuses' but were in fact using phony, bell-curve-style mathematics, while managing to convince themselves that it was great science, and thus turning the entire financial establishment into suckers."[49]

Had we only seen the real pattern in play, we would have realized that LTCM was the harbinger for much of the financial follies, including the derivatives failures, that we are living with today.

This brings us to the biggest problem facing *visionaries prix fixe*— their inability to predict the really, really big surprises. These are the "black swans" that Nassim Taleb writes about in his book *The Black*

Swan—the unforeseen events that have a habit of arriving when we think life is on a roll and there are no surprises ahead. Taleb's term refers to the discovery of black swans during the European exploration of Australia. Prior to that the existence of black swans was unanticipated, and so came as a great surprise to ornithologists.

If forecasters are at least good in forecasting the continuum (and they usually are), they fail abjectly in the face of a black swan. Every crisis imaginable—the Great Depression, 9/11, the derivatives collapse, subprime housing, the BP spill—were black swans.

To be sure, forecasters can nail the future when it comes to the short term, or when it comes to the general details. Or even when it comes to the general direction in which events will move. And in this, they serve a useful and admirable purpose, and should receive all the money and honor that they can scoop up. But it's the long shot (and this can be anywhere from a day to years depending on the circumstances) they often claim mastery over, and in which they usually fail.

So have we disproved the notion that visionaries can see into the future? Are visionaries, like *visionaries prix fixe,* merely focusing on streaks of randomness disguised as meaningful patterns? Perhaps they are merely lucky—as lucky as the money managers who hit their numbers and get on the cover of *Barron's* magazine.

But I don't think so. Visionaries are cut from an entirely different cloth than *visionaries prix fixe.* First, they don't make a business of forecasting. They forecast to *shape* the future, not merely to predict it. After all, as Alan Kay, the architect of the graphical user interface common to most computers, noted, "The best way to predict the future is to invent it."

As we have seen earlier, real visionaries don't assemble a massive bank of data. They know that data are in the past. Their story is always leaning forward. They think intuitively because the facts simply don't exist. And logic is not their forte—passion is. They are nothing like the well-heeled expert, arguing a point on TV. They are much more like the little boy at the parade, noticing that the emperor is not wearing any clothes.

"I have always lived my life thriving on opportunity and adventure," Richard Branson once noted. "Some of the best ideas come out of the blue, and you just have to keep an open mind to see their virtue."[50] Remember, it was Branson who insisted that Virgin register a trademark for Virgin Galactic Airways in 1994, while he was expanding his airline. That crazy prediction was made *years* ago. And today—to everyone's astonishment—it's about to become true.

10

CHAPTER TEN

Can You Learn Vision?

In the film *Field of Dreams,* Kevin Costner's character is walking through the cornfields when he hears a voice whispering, "Build it and they will come." The voice is insistent enough that Costner does indeed build it—a baseball field, in the middle of nowhere. He faces ridicule. His in-laws betray him. The bankers foreclose on his farm. But the tumblers of fate finally click into place. In the film's final scene, they do come—a line of cars as far as the eye can see, thousands of them—to share the visionary's dream.

On October 4, 2004, more than 20,000 people drove out into the blinding New Mexico desert to a remote landing strip. Dozens of television news trucks, satellite dishes deployed, were there as well. The man they all wanted to see was Burt Rutan, the rangy, irreverent aviation maverick. Rutan had built a spaceship—and now the crowds had gathered to watch it perform.

All of this was in response to a St. Louis–based initiative, partly funded by Microsoft co-founder Paul Allen, called the Ansari X PRIZE—a check for $10 million to the first person to send a commercial spaceship into space and bring it back in one piece. Early on, Burt Rutan was not anyone's guess to win the prize. When *Wired* wrote an article four years earlier about the race into space, the usually prescient magazine hadn't even included Rutan's name in the article. He was that far off the radar screen.[1]

But now *SpaceShipOne*—essentially the same craft that Burt Rutan had sketched out for me in his office four years earlier—was ready to go. She would be carried to the first 50,000 feet under the belly of the mother ship, called the *White Knight*. Then she would be released and rocket 60 miles straight up into the darkness of space.

They took off in the early morning light. Those in the crowd stretched their necks to see the tiny sparkle of light they made against the bright blue sky.

On the ground there was another visionary with whom you are now familiar: Richard Branson, who craned his neck along with everyone else. Less than a month earlier, Rutan had agreed to sell the rights to his spaceship technology to Virgin, pending the outcome of the flights and the winning of the X PRIZE.

At 50,000 feet *SpaceShipOne* separated from the mother ship and fell a few hundred yards. Then the rocket engine kicked in. At nearly 3,000 miles per hour, *SpaceShipOne* was pushed into the edge of space. Beyond the range of the naked eye she made a graceful, 15-minute arc of weightlessness, and was then pulled gently back to earth, like a badminton shuttlecock, the greens and blues of our planet spreading out below her.[2]

As she descended back into the atmosphere, sparkling again in the sunlight, Branson surely must have imagined how grand she would look henceforth, with a big red Virgin logo adorning her fuselage, the same logo that Branson had agreed to ("That'll do") on the pub napkin 30 years earlier.

Rutan did win the X PRIZE, and the check for $10 million. Even better, Branson pledged $100 million to turn Rutan's vision into a commercial enterprise. Work began immediately on a bigger, better spacecraft, *SpaceShipTwo,* with seating for six, more room to float around in weightlessness, and larger portholes for viewing the earth below. Today, Virgin has tickets to ride (if you want to get onboard, go to the Virgin Galactic Web site at www.galactica journeys.com), where about 300 travelers have already signed up at $200,000 a ride. Branson has said that Virgin Galactic plans to send more travelers into space in its first year of flight (slated for 2012) than have ever have been there before (that would be slightly more than 500). Virgin is even building a sleek passenger lounge at its "Spaceport America" in the New Mexico desert. And talk about déjà vu—it looks suspiciously like Eero Saarinen's iconic TWA terminal at Kennedy International Airport in New York, circa 1962.

Visionaries have all the luck. It comes together so easily for them, it seems, in a neat little package tied with a bright red ribbon. Most geniuses have been dealt a hand of four aces when it comes to genes, says psychologist Steven Pinker.[3] The same could be said of visionaries: Visionaries are born with the emotional intelligence card, the intuition card, the visualization card—and even the luck card. It's enough to make you fold your hand and walk away.

But hold on there. The good news is that neither geniuses nor visionaries are oddities of nature. They have the same restless, pattern-hunting brains as the rest of us. And there's even better news: Brain scientists now realize that human brains are not fixed by innate ability. As neuroscientists Steven Quartz and Terrence Sejnowski write, "The world helped construct your mind's circuits when you were growing up, and it continually reshapes them as you experience new things and call on new skills."[4]

In other words, the brain is not a fixed structure that processes what it receives; it is an ever-changing network of circuitry that learns and evolves as we live our lives.

I'm in a lab at the University of Miami, holding up to the light what might be considered a celebrity in the field of neuroscience. It's wet and slimy-looking at first glance, but as I raise it in my cupped hands I am surprised at how firm it is (I use the word "it," but it could be a he or a she). Oh dear, I must have upset it, because it's emitting a purple dye that's running down my arm. "Don't get that on your shirt," my host warns, handing me a paper towel. "You'll have a devil of a time getting it out."

What I'm holding is *Aplysia californica,* a herbivorous marine mollusk that is playing a critical role in the investigation of the brain. While human brains have 100 billion neurons, *Aplysia* has but 20,000. And they are *big* neurons—you can see them easily with a microscope. Even better, if you want to see *Aplysia* thinking and learning, you can even pick a cluster as small as 400 neurons and literally watch it happen.

This was the huge, Nobel Prize–winning breakthrough that Columbia University neuroscientist Eric Kandel and his colleagues gave the world a few years ago. They were the first to actually *see* *Aplysia*'s neurons creating new synapse connections (they applied light shocks to *Aplysia*'s tail and watched the neurons form new synaptic connections in anticipation of the next one). The experiment proved that learning has a biological basis, and conversely, that biology (the creation of new neuron patterns) is behind what we do and how we feel. In the case of *Aplysia,* it doubled the number of neuron connections as it learned to anticipate the shock. As for humans? Well, if you sit down and *really* practice your piano *every day* (as your mother told you to), your brain will create new synapse connections between the neurons to help you along.[5]

This is great news, because even though the number of neurons in the human brain decreases as we age (as has been said time and again), the number of *synaptic connections* can grow as long as we live. If we keep using our noodle, in other words, we can make our brain better every day.

But Kandel's research goes a significant step beyond that: Using your brain not only increases your synaptic connections, it also changes what was once thought to be unchangeable: our *genes*. "If you give it [*Aplysia*] repeated shocks, something astonishing happens," Kandel explains. "The signaling system goes into the nucleus where the genes are located and it turns on gene expression." He continues, "We had thought that the genes are the governors of behavior, the determinants of behavior. But what our experiments suggested is that behavior can act on genes to regulate the expression. So genes are not only the controllers of the behavior, they are also the servants of the environment."[6]

In other words, if you've had a conversation with a friend, and you remember it the next day, you have not only created new synapse connections, but also anatomically changed your brain—and your genetic makeup as well. More recent research even suggests that some of that genetic improvement can be transferred down to your future generations.

That is a startling and controversial finding, but Kandel's discoveries are finding agreement. Say neuroscientists Quartz and Sejnowski, "Being born some way doesn't amount to being forever to remain that way . . . Your experiences with the world alter your brain's structure, chemistry, and genetic expression, often profoundly, throughout your life." Says New York University neurologist LeDoux, "Learning allows us to transcend our genes."[7]

And that's why *Aplysia* are such celebrities in the world of neuroscience. Scientists worldwide are studying their neurons. Experimenters at the Salk Institute, for instance, are using modified rabies viruses to infiltrate cells and move across synapses. Because the virus is engineered to produce green fluorescent protein (thanks in great part to the work of our Mr. Prasher), the scientists can watch it move from neuron to neuron, thus mapping every single neuron that connects to a particular cell.

Little wonder that the University of Miami Rosenstiel School of Marine and Atmospheric Science is raising some 30,000 *Aplysia* a year and shipping them to researchers around the world.[8] *Aplysia* has become the most useful research animal since the laboratory mouse.

But if we can change our brains—improving them—how do we do that? Piano lessons are not enough. We need to start *thinking* about the way we think, so we can understand what's going on when we awaken to a new pattern, feel the tug of intuition, visualize something clearly, or even experience a run of "luck." The term for this process of reflection is "metacognition," first coined by psychologist John Flavell in 1976. In a sense, metacognition is the flip side of intuition. Where intuition is unconscious and free-form, metacognition is careful and conscious. It is the ability to listen to one's intellect and emotions. It is thinking *about* our thinking.

So what are the lessons of the visionaries that we can ponder and put to use for ourselves?

Awakening

Think back to the last time that something "dawned" on you. We've all had the experience. Perhaps you suddenly realize that your job is no longer rewarding. Or that the road you always take to get back home isn't actually the fastest. Think back to the last time you had a good idea. The response is fast: The lightbulb snaps on. The next time that happens, make note of it.

Remember, too, that in our daily lives we stroll through

billowing clouds of silk, aware of the vague patterns of life around us, but little else. The "gist," they call it. So we walk around getting the gist of things, but we rarely open our eyes. Think back to the gorilla walking between the basketball players. That will remind you that we too often focus on the details, and miss the big picture.

Remember as well the lesson of Clairol, in which the level of thinking is raised from the mundane to the inspired. Clairol is what? A chemical. Higher? It makes your hair blonde. Higher than that? Blondes have more fun.

Seeing

It was not too long ago that people would gather around the radio to listen to a ball game. Was there any less excitement because the game was being played essentially in their heads rather than before their eyes? The most important thing to remember is that the brain has given us the great gift of visualization. Innovation is made even better because we can not only fix images in our mind's eye, we can also shuffle around the parts—or add things that are entirely new. (And it's not only objects that we can move around in our mind's eye, but concepts as well.) Think back to Jeff Hawkins and his invention of the PalmPilot. Or the example of Elmer Sperry, whose visual sense was so strong that he would hold a pad of paper in the air and draw what his mind was seeing. Think of that incredible meeting between Edwin Land and Steve Jobs, when they both saw their creations floating between them above the conference room table.

Visualization is a skill you can learn, and fortunately, it is being taught in schools more and more frequently. Math departments are returning to visual training. So are engineering schools, where computer-aided design had discouraged the use of one's inner vision to design things. Meanwhile, audiobooks are filling commuters' cars with mental images. "Fortunately, imaging skills can be learned and improved by exercise," note Robert and Michele Root-Bernstein in their classic book *Sparks of Genius*. "The abilities of observing, imaging, dimensional thinking, modeling, synthesizing are standard equipment in the brain," they add. "All you must do is turn them on."[9]

Intuition

Without a doubt, intuition is the critical skill that visionaries employ. How else can they make those incredible calls—like Jobs trimming the Apple lineup to a handful of computers, or Branson deciding within an hour or so to get into the airline business? But the lesson we've learned is that intuition is a two-edged sword. A "hunch" or "gut feeling" can be disastrous.

Intuition seems to work best when one is well-versed in the subject matter. Dr. Jerome Groopman, author of the best seller *How Doctors Think,* writes, "Clinical intuition is a complex sense that becomes refined over years and years of practice, of listening to literally thousands of patients' stories, examining thousands of people, and most important, remembering when you were wrong."[10] And recall that, as Gerd Gigerenzer has observed, intuitions based on one good reason tend to be accurate—but only under certain conditions: when one has to predict the future, when the future is difficult to foresee, and when one has only limited information. If you are trying to decide between the $15 and $25 car wash, it makes sense to rationally compare the services you get for each. But if you are trying to decide between the Audi on one car lot and the Mercedes on the other, reams of information won't make it easier. In any case, a middle-road approach is best: Studies of professional poker players show that they pull from both sides of the equation, going with their gut sometimes but not completely, and using reason when reason seems to be making the best call.

Courage and Conviction

We now know the difference between dreamers and real business visionaries: blood, sweat, and tears; the evolutionary thrashing of the tail against relentlessly opposing currents; a preference for those places, as Andy Grove put it, where "only the paranoid survive."

But for someone willing to put in the effort, there is some consolation. We've learned from Thomas Kuhn that the burst of paradigms is followed by years of reverberations. It's in this period of "mopping up," as he terms it, that opportunities abound. You might say we are still mopping up from the social networking burst; step farther back and you could say we are still mopping up from the birth of the Internet. Farther back still and we are still mopping up from the PC revolution; farther back than that, and we are still mopping up from the invention of the semiconductor. A hundred years from now, the last 400 years may be known simply as the Electric Age, in which we mopped up from the discoveries of William Gilbert, Otto von Guericke, Luigi Galvani, and the other pioneers of electricity. The point here is that few business visionaries pull their ideas out of thin air; they have merely picked the point at which they will do some mopping up.

Another consolation is that you've got company. As noted earlier, the Wright brothers built their success on the shoulders of many others, and in fact they probably would have failed had they attempted their *Flyer* even a few years earlier. Similarly, Thomas Edison invented the phonograph based on the failed noodlings of Alexander Graham Bell (which employed a cadaver's ear; imagine stereo!). In turn, Bell based his experiments largely on the work of a long-forgotten inventor named Édouard-Léon Scott de

Martinville. As Julian Huxley reminded us, it's the nature of technological invention that many people will be working on the same
problem not only sequentially but simultaneously. That's why it's
critical to keep one's eyes open and rub elbows with those who are
undertaking interesting work. Just ask Steve Jobs, who saw the
future of the PC when he visited Xerox PARC and finally saw their
graphical user interface and computer mouse.

Scaling up the Vision

No matter how solitary and boarded up a visionary may be
emotionally, he or she has to get other people onboard in order to
make the dream succeed. At Intel, former chairman Bob Noyce has
been credited with building the firm through his charm as well
as his technical genius (he was a coinventor of the semiconductor). Still, Noyce was "approachable the first inch, and after that
you don't go any farther," noted his colleague Andy Grove. Most
visionaries fit that description, whether they are Walt Disney or
Steve Jobs.

But it's this outer inch of charm that makes all the difference.
It helps raise money and build a staff. A big part of emotional
intelligence has to do with visualization—this time a perspective
on people, rather than things. "First of all," Atticus Finch told his
daughter in *To Kill a Mockingbird,* "if you can learn a simple trick,
Scout, you'll get along a lot better with all kinds of folks. You never
really understand a person until you consider things from his point
of view—"[11]

That is one of the big lessons that can be drawn from the lives of
visionaries—they can read people, get under their skin, and with
that knowledge, add them to the team. The metacognition training that is now becoming part of medical school curriculums, for
instance, is teaching doctors to *think* like a patient. It is not enough
to ask what it's like to be diabetic. You need to ask what it's like to

be a diabetic who is losing her home to foreclosure. Thinking like another person is not merely a matter of sensitivity; it is a way to read symptoms and seek cures.

Some people are born with more emotional intelligence than others. In most visionaries, I would venture to say, it's instinctive. But fortunately emotional intelligence can be taught. By simply recognizing the elements of emotional intelligence and putting them to practice, people can increase their own share of it. Back in the 1920s Dale Carnegie recognized this, and popularized his take on the emotional skills required of leadership. Since its initial publication, his *How to Win Friends and Influence People* has never been out of print. If you search the book on Amazon.com today, you'll see some 700 customer comments—most offering five-star reviews. Emotional intelligence today, be it the Carnegie model or that springing from Goleman's best seller, can be taught—from negotiating skills to the ability to control one's anger.

Luck

Luck is random and mysterious, but it is not unattainable. How? By simply staying in the game. "What I've learned, above all," says *Drunkard's Walk* author Leonard Mlodinow, "is to keep marching forward—because the best news is that since chance does play a role, one important factor in success is under our control: the number of at-bats, the number of chances taken, the number of opportunities seized. For even a coin weighted toward failure will sometimes land on success."[12]

But it's not just hard work that favors luck. Attitude counts for a lot of it. That was underscored in a study by Richard Wiseman, a psychologist at the University of Hertfordshire. Wiseman surveyed a number of people and, through a series of questionnaires and interviews, determined which of them considered themselves lucky—or unlucky. He then performed a fascinating experiment:

He gave both the "lucky" and "unlucky" people a newspaper, and asked them to look through it and tell him how many photographs were inside. He found that, on average, the unlucky people took two minutes to count all the photographs, whereas the lucky ones determined the number in seconds. How could the lucky people do this? Because they quickly found a message on the second page that read, "Stop counting. There are 43 photographs in this newspaper." So why didn't the unlucky people see this? Because they were so intent on counting all the photographs, they missed the message! Wiseman offers this explanation: "Unlucky people miss chance opportunities because they are too focused on looking for something else. They go to parties intent on finding their perfect partner, and so miss opportunities to make good friends. They look through newspapers determined to find certain types of job advertisements and as a result miss other types of jobs. Lucky people are more relaxed and open, and therefore see what is there rather than just what they are looking for."

Other characteristics of lucky people, he noted, are that they tend to follow their intuition, whereas unlucky ones rely overly on rational thought. Also, he says, unlucky people "tend to be creatures of routine," whereas lucky people thrive on variety. Lucky people see the positive side to any ill fortune. On one occasion, Wiseman recalls, one of his lucky participants arrived with his leg in a cast. Wiseman asked him if he still felt lucky. "He cheerfully explained that he felt even luckier than before," Wiseman noted. "As he pointed out, he could have broken his neck."[13]

Sure, some people are born with an attitude that favors luck. And some of us are not. But fortunately, a good attitude—one that favors luck—is not out of reach. "Optimism and hope, like helplessness and despair, can be learned," says *Emotional Intelligence* author Goleman.

Here's another image that might help you increase your luck: Think about catching a ball that is hit deep into center field. How is the catch made? Luck rarely drops the ball into the pocket of the glove. Nor does the fielder's brain instantly calculate the distance, velocity, and projection of the ball, not to mention the air resistance, the wind speed, and the spin that influence its flight. The human brain can't do that. So how does the fielder make the miraculous catch? Simply by running toward it with glove extended. And guess what: As the fielder runs forward, the brain is making on-the-run adjustments—reading-adjusting, reading-adjusting, reading-adjusting, until—*fwap!*—the ball lands in the pocket of the glove. That is exactly the right metaphor for luck: If you keep running toward it, stay loose, keep readjusting yourself, and never give up, you have the best chance of landing the ball in your glove.[14]

That's why visionaries never hobble themselves with preconceived notions. They'd prefer *not* to know precisely where they'll wind up next. When Branson opened his first Virgin record store in London, he didn't know that he'd eventually end up with a spaceship. He just ran fast, adjusting his plans whenever necessary. When Diane von Furstenberg invented her wrap dress, she never realized that she'd be making more money with her signature brand than with that particular design. Walt Disney never dreamed of full-length feature animations, let alone theme parks. "The length of my foresight is measured by this admission: Even as late as 1930, my ambition was to be able to make cartoons as good as the Aesop's Fables series," he once said.[15] Like the fielder chasing the ball, these visionaries simply kept running forward, adjusting their ambition along the way.

"All we can do is to encourage the conditions from which it can emerge." Taleb says of luck. "The reason free markets work is because they allow people to be lucky, thanks to aggressive trial and error, not by giving rewards or incentives for skill. The strategy is, then, to tinker as much as possible and try to collect as many Black Swan opportunities as you can."[16]

Visionaries that make it big enough end up on magazine covers and on TV. But they are hardly the only visionaries. We are surrounded by visionaries of one kind or another. Let me repeat the thought by philosopher Eckhart Tolle, who notes that visionaries are people "that function from the deeper core of their being—those who do not attempt to appear more than they are, but as simply themselves, stand out as remarkable, and are the only ones who truly make a difference in the world." He adds, "Their mere presence, simple, natural and unassuming, has a transformational effect on whomever they come into contact with."[17] A very good point—and one that leads me to my final story.

When Fred Woodward was twenty-two years old, he made his way from Noxapater, Mississippi (population 500), to Memphis, Tennessee, where he took up graphic design at Memphis State University. On the side, he assisted the art director at the *City of Memphis* magazine, and when the art director quit, Fred dropped out of college and took his place. The magazine was housed in a prefab metal building in an industrial strip, with a few wooden desks upstairs and a printing press rumbling below.

That's where I met Fred about a year later, when I became the magazine's managing editor (which entitled me to a desk made of two boards and a beaten-up Royal typewriter). Fred and I quickly became friends. We went to parties together. And it wasn't long before Fred confided in me an audacious aspiration: to become the art director of *Rolling Stone* magazine.

To say the least, some people didn't take Fred or his dream seriously (in fact, his counselor at Memphis State had suggested that Fred "turn around and go back to Mississippi). But back in the darkroom of the magazine, where the pages were shot to be made into plates and put on the press, he caught the attention of a fellow named Jack Nunnally, and Fred's life began to change, perhaps unbeknownst to Fred himself.

Jack was a wiry cat. He combed his white hair straight back into a fifties-era ducktail. And he wore the thickest Coke-bottle eyeglasses you ever saw. You'd find Jack in that darkroom night and day, bathed in red light, glasses flashing like strobes as he shot the pages. But there was something else that you quickly learned about Jack. He had been a jazz drummer, and he loved that groove. And so Jack was rarely alone in his lair. He had his friends spinning on the cassettes in his portable tape player—Ella, Miles, Dizzy, Thelonious, and more.

Jack delighted in being around the twenty-somethings who were putting out the magazine. The publisher, Bob Towery, was "a solid stud" (an influential man); Bob's wife Patty was "a shape in a drape" (looking good); my fellow editor Ed Weathers and I "dug those mellow kicks" (knew how to live). Editor Ken DeCell was "really in there" (knew all the answers).

But Fred—Jack really dug Fred. He'd tell Fred all about his days as a jazz drummer, and listen to Fred talk about *Rolling Stone.* And then Jack bestowed upon Fred about as big an honor as Jack could bestow upon anyone: Every week he'd have a couple of his precious jazz albums ready for Fred. Those precious thirty-three-and-a-thirds. And he'd let Fred take them home for a listen. That was *big.*

So what happened? Over the course of four years Fred and his assistant art director, Murry Keith, won several design awards for their work at *Memphis* magazine. Then Fred moved on to *D* magazine, the city magazine of Dallas. He won more awards there. Then it was on to the *Dallas Morning News,* and finally a dream job, as art director of the prestigious *Texas Monthly.*

After four years of winning design awards for *Texas Monthly,* Fred made a jump to a glossy Washington, D.C., magazine named *Regardie's.* To most of us, *Regardie's* was a big step down from *Texas Monthly.* But to Fred, it was geographically closer to his goal— New York City.

Then one afternoon, as I was pounding out a story for the *Wall Street Journal,* I received a panicked call from Fred. He had just been asked by Jann Wenner—the publisher of *Rolling Stone*—to become their new art director. "What should I do?" Fred asked. "Are you kidding?" I replied. "From day one, you said you wanted to be the art director of *Rolling Stone.*" "Yes, but I just started at *Regardie's.*" "Fred, you have one chance. Go for it."

Heeding my advice, and doubtlessly that of others, Fred did. He made the big leap to the Big Apple—or more specifically, to the looming Fifth Avenue mansion that housed *Rolling Stone.* Fred went on to art direct *Rolling Stone* for 15 award-winning years, also becoming the creative director of the entire company, overseeing *Men's Journal, Us, Rolling Stone,* and the company's book-publishing interest. In 1996 Fred became the youngest inductee ever into the Art Directors Hall of Fame. "Fred is a true visionary," Wenner said at the black-tie dinner. In 2001 Fred took another big leap— becoming the design director of *GQ* magazine, where he is today. Not a bad run. But that's the power of vision.[18]

In early 2010 Fred sent me a boxed set of six CDs. I have them sitting on my desk next to my laptop right now. The collecton is called *Jack's Darkroom Music.* It contains some of Jack's favorite tunes, lovingly hand-picked by Fred: Count Basie, Gerry Mulligan, Carmen McRae, Charlie Parker, Billie Holiday—they're all there. Fred designed a different cover for each CD, featuring a black-and-white photo of a different jazz star. "Jack Nunnally was the original hipster," Fred wrote in the liner notes, "wiry and hyperkinetic— a whole mess of swagger wound up real tight." Fred continued, "When I first met Jack, I was 'a square' (corn-fed) lad of 21, but under his tutelage—he would always whisper, 'Dig what I'm putting down, Freddy'—I soon enough became 'a cat.'"

Fred learned from Jack. "He helped me realize that great art could come from improvisation," Fred told me, "that it was okay to loosen up, stop being insecure about my lack of education, and stop copying and just trust my gut that my first idea was often the best idea."

It's more than that, though. Jack saw what Fred had to offer—where he was destined to go. Through those Coke-bottle glasses, Jack could see the future better than all of us combined.

And so for everything that Fred has accomplished in *his* career, we now know the truth—and we wish we had said it to Jack when he was still around: Jack was a visionary too.

ACKNOWLEDGMENTS

My first thanks go to David Moldawer, who not only skillfully edited this book but also came up with the idea for a book on visionaries. I don't know if David sat bolt upright in bed with it (as visionaries sometimes do), but his idea was a great one, and I thank him for it. My thanks also to Cathy Dexter, the book's copy editor, whose keen eye and insightful suggestions helped me enormously.

I'd like to thank Jeff Stibel for leading me to the works of Daniel Dennett, Steven Pinker, and other essential brain-science thinkers, and Dan Ariely for introducing me to the works of Daniel Kahneman and cognitive psychology in general. The bibliography that follows lists dozens of books. You'll know my favorites because I cite them frequently. But every one of those books is worth reading; they served as the stepping-stones that led me through this journey.

Since so many of the stories in this book spring from my years at the *Wall Street Journal* and *Fortune,* I want to express my gratitude to those who made those experiences possible: John Huey, who made the decision to hire me at the *Journal* in the first place; and Larry O'Donnell for green-lighting that hire; Norm Pearlstine for sending me to the London bureau; and London bureau chief Phil Revzin as well as deputy bureau chiefs Larry Ingrassia and George Anders, who encouraged me as I trekked across Europe in search of stories. You couldn't ask for a better group of writers, editors, or friends. At *Fortune* I was hired by the legendary editor Marshall Loeb and later worked with his successor, John Huey, who let me pursue stories of my own invention, which led me to Steve Jobs, Andy Grove, and many of the visionaries described in this book.

Further thanks go to the PIPs, for puffing away politely during my brain-science monologues; Dr. Carl Geier of the I'On book club and Dr. Anthony Bishara of the College of Charleston for their comments and suggestions; George Getschow and the tribe of writers at the Mayborn Literary Nonfiction Conference for their support; Billy Collins for the invitation to give my first "Ten Steps Ahead" talk; Barbara Hagerty for my inclusion in her Charleston writers' salon; Loren Ziff for the use of the beachside office; Jack Alterman for the fine photo; and the College of Charleston for the use of their excellent library.

I especially want to thank my agents, Jim Levine and Danielle Svetcov, who brought this project to me, and to particularly thank Danielle for working with me to make the book proposal sing.

At Portfolio I worked with a great team of professionals, including my publicist, Laura Clark, and Emily Angell and Barbara Campo on the editorial side.

Finally, I want to thank my wife, Nancy, and my son, Matthew, for spending another year with a writer who is paddling through the fog to a distant beacon. Their love and support made this book possible.

NOTES

Full publishing information for books cited in these notes can be found in the bibliography.

INTRODUCTION

1. Richard Branson, *Losing My Virginity* (2007 edition), 467.

2. To secure your ticket, go to www.Virgingalactic.com or www .Galacticajourneys.com.

CHAPTER 1: The Elements of Vision

1. Erik Calonius, "Garages," *Fortune,* March 4, 1996.

2. Erik Calonius, "Their Wildest Dreams," *Fortune,* August 15, 1999.

3. Branson, *Losing My Virginity,* 345.

4. In writing this exceedingly brief history, I am grateful for Carl Zimmer's absorbing history of medicine (and brain science) in *Soul Made Flesh.*

5. Pinker, *How the Mind Works,* 22.

6. From the Brain Science Podcast, www.brainsciencepodcast.com. This series, hosted by Dr. Ginger Campbell, offers fascinating interviews with leaders in brain science and cognitive psychology.

7. Descriptions of this remarkable convergence upon brain science can be found in Montague's *Your Brain Is (Almost) Perfect,* 15, and Quartz and Sejnowski's *Liars, Lovers and Heroes,* 23.

8. Jim Thornton, "Understanding a Broken Heart," *Men's Health,* April 19, 2009.

9. This history of brain research is well detailed in Doidge, *The Brain That Changes Itself,* 16.

10. Damasio, *Looking for Spinoza,* 67.

11. See more about the development of the MRI in Berns, *Iconoclast,* 26.

12. Dr. Raymond Damadian is also credited with developing the MRI machine, and a bitter dispute erupted when the Nobel Prize was awarded to Dr. Lauterbur. See Kenneth Change, "Denied Nobel for MRI, He Wins Another Prize," *New York Times,* March 23, 2004.

13. There is now an MRI machine for every 40,000 Americans, a number that has caused criticism and fears of its overuse. See Mark Gimein, "The Machine That Is Bankrupting America," September 21, 2009, www.thebigmoney.com/articles/money-trail/2009/09/21.

14. For a complete and very readable history of Turing, von Neumann, and other pioneers in the development of artificial intelligence, I would recommend James Hogan's *Mind Matters.* For more on Turing, see Montague, *Your Brain Is (Almost) Perfect,* and the section on AI in Dennett, *Consciousness Explained.*

15. Dennett, *Consciousness Explained,* 212.

16. John von Neumann, "First Draft of a Report on the EDVAC," June 30, 1945.

17. Pinker, *How the Mind Works,* 137.

18. Koch, *The Quest for Consciousness,* 48.

CHAPTER 2: Awakening

1. Erik Calonius, "Flying High: How Richard Branson of Virgin Group Is a Star of Music and Films, and Now Runs an Airline," *Wall Street Journal,* August 8, 1984, p. 1.

2. Branson, *Losing My Virginity,* 62.

3. This wasn't the only time that Branson's attention turned from the music at hand. In his autobiography (p. 91) he notes, "When 'Tubular Bells' started, I was lying on the sofa . . . I could see everyone else lying around totally spellbound by the music. But I kept worrying. I find it impossible to stop my brain from churning through all the ideas and possibilities facing me at any given moment . . ."

4. Pinker, *How the Mind Works,* 88.

5. For more on Miller, see Stibel, *Wired for Thought,* 90, as well as LeDoux, *Synaptic Self,* 175; and Newberg and Waldman, *Why We Believe What We Believe,* 30.

6. Myers, *Intuition,* 54.

7. David Myers notes in *Intuition* (p. 56), "Novices see information in isolated pieces; experts see large meaningful patterns."

8. Polykoff, *Does She or Doesn't She?* 26.

9. Chabris and Simons, *The Invisible Gorilla,* 5. Also see "Gorillas in Our Midst: Sustained Inattentional Blindness to Dynamic Events," *Perception,*

vol. 28 (1999), 1059. Also, Dr. Robert Burton describes his reaction to the gorilla video in Burton, *On Being Certain,* 154. See also Ronald A. Rensink et al., "To See or Not to See," *Psychological Science,* vol. 8, no. 5, September 1997.

10. Chabris and Simons, *The Invisible Gorilla,* 7. See also Hanson, *Perception and Discovery,* 61.

11. From *Tales of Mother Goose.* Dr. Robert Burton offers his own clever riddle, and an analysis, on p. 5 of *On Being Certain.*

12. Quotes are from Taleb, *The Black Swan,* 225.

13. Branson, *Losing My Virginity,* 190.

CHAPTER 3: Seeing

1. Ferguson, *Engineering and the Mind's Eye,* xi, 42.

2. Koch, *Quest,* 29.

3. Damasio, *Descartes' Error,* 102.

4. Shah and Miyake, *Cambridge Handbook of Visuospatial Thinking,* 43.

5. Gazzaniga, *Human,* 187.

6. Shah, *Cambridge Handbook,* 42.

7. Sacks, *The Man Who Mistook His Wife for a Hat,* 16.

8. Damasio, *Descartes' Error,* 106. Einstein once noted, "Words have to be sought in the second state. The thought—often visual—comes first."

9. Kosslyn and Koenig, *Wet Mind,* 144.

10. Dennett, *Consciousness Explained,* 135.

11. Bernstein, *Sparks of Genius,* 58.

12. Ferguson, *Engineering and the Mind's Eye,* 51. Also see Thomas Hughes, *Elmer Sperry, Inventor and Engineer* (Baltimore: Johns Hopkins University Press, 1977).

13. Gabler, *Walt Disney: The Triumph of the American Imagination,* 164.

14. Erik Calonius, "The Rivals: Competition for Glory and Money Is Fierce in Big Time Science," *Wall Street Journal,* December 28, 1984, p. 1.

15. Wolpert and Richards, *Passionate Minds,* 198.

16. Ibid., 126.

17. Bernstein, *Sparks of Genius,* 196.

18. Galton, *Inquiries into Human Faculty and Understanding.* See also Shah, *Cambridge Handbook,* 62, and Hunter, *Memory,* 189.

19. Shah, *Cambridge Handbook,* 62.

20. Erik Calonius, "Their Wildest Dreams," *Fortune,* August 16, 1999.

21. For additional background on Hawkins, I'm indebted to Andrea Butter and David Pogue's *Piloting Palm: The Inside Story of Palm, Handspring and the Birth of the Billion Dollar Handheld Industry.*

22. Zimmer, *Soul Made Flesh,* 73.

23. Jakab, *Visions of a Flying Machine,* 6.

24. Noe, *Out of Our Heads,* 60.

25. Young and Simon, *iCon,* 60.

26. Ferguson, *Engineering and the Mind's Eye,* 169.

27. Ibid., 164.

28. Ibid., 143, 150.

29. Feynman, *Surely You're Joking, Mr. Feynman!* 173.

30. Victor McElheny, *Biographical Memories: Herbert Land,* National Academies Press.

31. Sculley, *Odyssey,* 155.

32. Kahney, *Inside Steve's Brain,* 178.

33. Sculley, *Odyssey,* 162.

CHAPTER 4: Intuition

1. Brent is now a partner in Techonomy, a leading Silicon Valley media firm, along with former *Fortune* senior writers David Kirkpatrick and Peter Petre. In 1994, Jobs expressed his emotions about Apple: "The MacIntosh was sort of like this wonderful romance in your life that you once had, and that produced about 10 million children," he told Jeff Goodell in the June 16, 1994, issue of *Rolling Stone.* "In a way it will never be over in your life. You still smell that romance every morning when you get up. And when you open the window, the cool air will hit your face, and you'll smell that romance in the air."

2. Burrows and Grover, "Steve Jobs' Magic Kingdom," *BusinessWeek,* February 6, 2006.

3. Deutschman, *The Second Coming of Steve Jobs,* 251.

4. This story is told in Kahney's *Inside Steve's Brain,* 29.

5. Quoted in Goldberg's *The Wisdom Paradox,* 152.

6. Branson, *Losing My Virginity,* 161.

7. Gabler, *Disney,* 220.

8. Hurlburt, *Describing Inner Experience;* also see Klein, *The Secret Pulse of Time,* 92.

9. Francis Galton, *Psychometric Experiments,* 149, galton.org/essays/1870-1879/galton-1879-brain-psychometric-experiments/galton-1879-brain-psychometric-experiments.pdf. The Pall Mall is the major thoroughfare through the St. James area of London.

10. Damasio, *Descartes' Error,* 111, 116.

11. Noe, *Out of Our Heads,* 56.

12. Klein, *Secret Pulse of Time,* 17, 42–47. In *Quest for Consciousness* (p. 39), Koch notes that when scientists amplify the electrical activity of neurons, they can hear them "whooshing" and "crackling."

13. Le Fanu, *The Rise and Fall of Modern Medicine,* 204.

14. Wilson, *Strangers to Ourselves,* 24.

15. Dennett, *Consciousness Explained,* 229.

16. Wilson, *Strangers to Ourselves,* 35.

17. Mamet, *Glengarry Glen Ross,* 31.

18. See Hogan, *Mind Matters,* 258, for much more on this.

19. Described in Malcolm Gladwell's *The Tipping Point* (New York: Little, Brown, 2007), 81.

20. Quartz, *Liars, Lovers and Heroes,* 18.

21. *Planet Earth,* "Shallow Seas" segment, BBC/Warner Bros.

22. Details are available in Gregory Berns et al., "Brain Regions Responsive to Novelty in the Absence of Awarenesss," *Science* 23, May 1997, 1272. Wilson, in *Strangers to Ourselves* (p. 66), notes that the brain's "adaptive unconsciousness" is an older system that detects patterns that we are not conscious of.

23. Damasio, *Descartes' Error,* 212.

24. Mayer and Salovey, "What Is Emotional Intelligence?" in *Emotional Intelligence: Key Readings,* 35.

25. Goleman, *Emotional Intelligence,* 23.

26. From David Brooks, "The Empathy Issue," *New York Times,* op-ed, May 29, 2009.

27. Gigerenzer, *Gut Feelings,* 28.

28. This is more fully described in Jonah Lehrer's insightful *How We Decide,* 159. The full study ("Predictive Efficiency of Two Multivariate Statistical Techniques") can be found in the *Journal of Educational Psychology* (1965), 297. Another study concludes that statistical techniques overall are 10 percent more accurate than clinical predictions (done by humans). See *Psychology Assessment,* 2000, no. 1, 19.

29. I've simplified Dijksterhuis's experiments, but in *How We Decide* (p. 232), Lehrer describes them in greater detail. The IKEA experiment is discussed on p. 268 of Gladwell's *Blink.* For the original study, see *Science,* vol. 311, February 17, 2006, 10005.

30. Ambady and Rosenthal, "Predicting Teacher Evaluations from Thin Slices of Nonverbal Behavior and Physical Attractiveness," *Journal of Personality and Social Psychology* 64 (1993), 431.

31. As described in Taleb, *The Black Swan,* 145.

32. Gigerenzer, *Gut Feelings,* 122, 151.

33. Taleb, *The Black Swan,* 144.

34. Branson, *Losing My Virginity,* 152.

35. Ibid., 154.

36. Mlodinow, *The Drunkard's Walk,* 4.

37. Chabris and Simons, *The Invisible Gorilla,* 231.

38. From Jeff Goodell, "Steve Jobs, The *Rolling Stone* Interview," *Rolling Stone,* June 16, 1994.

39. *Beatles Anthology* (New York: Chronicle Books, 2000), 196.

40. Bernstein, *Sparks of Genius,* 61; also Kuhn, *The Structure of Scientific Revolutions,* 122.

41. Wolpert, *Passionate Minds,* 200.

42. Judson, *The Search for Solutions,* 24.

43. Wolpert, *Passionate Minds,* 200.

44. Montague, *Your Brain Is (Almost) Perfect,* 108.

45. Judson, *The Search for Solutions,* 70.

46. From a speech at *Popular Mechanics* magazine's "Breakthrough Leadership Award" conference, October 6, 2006 (www.popularmechanics.com/science/space/news/4199393?nav-RSS20).

47. Taleb, *The Black Swan,* 170.

CHAPTER 5: Courage and Conviction

1. Gabler, *Walt Disney,* 100.

2. Ibid., 162.

3. Thomas, *An American Original,* 104.

4. Galber, *Walt Disney,* 164.

5. Ibid.

6. Erik Calonius, "Working Dangerously," *Fortune,* October 14, 1996.

7. Ibid.

8. Erik Calonius, "Their Wildest Dreams," *Fortune,* August 16, 1999.

9. Ibid. Also draws information from Diane von Furstenberg, *Diane: A Signature Life,* as well as Joyce Maynard, "The Princess Who Has Everything," *New York Times,* February 16, 1977.

10. Montague, *Your Brain Is (Almost) Perfect,* 107, 113. The original study (in the 1970s) was performed by Wolfram Schultz. Burton, in *On Being Certain,* (p. 98), says that a need for dopamine may make certain individuals take risks.

11. Klein, *The Science of Happiness,* 88, 103.

12. Gabler, *Walt Disney,* 188.

13. This is from the great series of interviews with Disney animators and directors conducted by Don Peri in *Working With Walt.* This particular one (p. 54) is with Clarence Nash, the voice of Donald Duck.

14. Ibid., 6.

15. Goldberg, *The Wisdom Paradox,* 230.

16. Damasio, *Descartes' Error,* 264.

17. Goleman, *Emotional Intelligence,* 22. In *The Paradox of Choice* (p. 152) Barry Schwartz states he has found that "counterfactual thinking (imagination) is often triggered by something unpleasant."

18. In *The Animated Man,* author Michael Barrier recounts that Walt Disney's father had become incensed because Walt had talked back to him, and ordered him into the basement for a thrashing. Walt recalled, "And he started to hit me. And I took the hammer out of his hand. He raised his other hand and I held both of his hands. And I just held them there. I was stronger than he was. And he cried. He never touched me after that." (Disney's father was strict, but at least by the standards of the times, and considering the poverty and hardship of their circumstances, was not intentionally abusive, with the exception of the hammer incident.)

19. Gabler, *Walt Disney,* 322.

20. This is decribed in Gary Taubes's *Nobel Dreams,* 23.

21. Branson, *Losing My Virginity,* 37.

22. Barrier, *Animated Man,* 131; Gabler, *Disney,* 271.

23. Von Furstenberg, *Diane: A Signature Life,* 57.

24. Young and Simon, *iCon,* 24–27.

25. Sculley, *Odyssey,* 90.

26. Price, *The Pixar Touch,* 83.

27. Erik Calonius, "On a Wing and a Prayer," *Fortune,* November 9, 1998. Also see Vera Rollo, *Burt Rutan: Reinventing the Airplane.*

28. Arp, *Scenario Visualizaton,* 134.

29. From *The Scientist:* See article and blog at www.the-scientist.com/blog/display/55771/. See also *Current Biology,* June 23, 2009, for complete study.

30. Huxley, *Knowledge, Morality and Destiny,* 22.

31. Ibid.

32. See Stibel, *Wired for Thought,* 24, for more about this.

33. Margaret Wertheim, "Niles Eldredge: Bursts of Cornets and Evolution," *New York Times,* March 9, 2004; also, Belinda Barnet, "Material Cultural Evolution: An Interview with Niles Eldredge," www.journal.fibreculture.org/issue3/issue3_barnet.html.

34. Daniel Lyons, "Why Bezos Was Surprised by Kindle's Success," Newsweek.com, December 21, 2009.

35. Thomas, *Walt Disney: An American Original,* 351.

36. Barrier, *The Animated Man,* 166.

CHAPTER 6: Scaling up the Vision

1. Our destination that day—the Scilly Isles (off the southwestern tip of Britain)—held a special significance for Branson: The nearby Bishop's Rock Lighthouse was the finish line for the "Blue Riband" transatlantic boat race, in which Branson and a crew of courageous men nearly died attempting to break the world transatlantic speed record (which had been set in 1952). Trying

again in 1986, aboard the 70-foot *Virgin Atlantic Challenger II,* they succeeded in beating the record (although they were denied the prize due to a technicality). See Branson's account of this on p. 169 of *Losing My Virginity.* Incidentally, I don't think my editors on the Branson story, London bureau chief Phil Revzin and deputy bureau chief Larry Ingrassia, knew that I was gallivanting about the skies with Branson that day (they probably thought I was working on that story about the Italian telephone system), so please don't tell them.

2. In *Linked: The New Science of Networks* (p. 85), network expert Albert-Laszlo Barabasi calls supernodes "hubs."

3. See Gladwell's clever use of Paul Revere's ride on p. 59 of *The Tipping Point.*

4. Christakis and Fowler, *Connected,* 30; also see Barabasi, *Linked,* 25, 58.

5. In *Linked* (p. 87) Barabasi says that hubs can create "scale-free networks" that can extend to the horizons.

6. For more on how this works, see Christakis and Fowler's excellent *Connected,* 157.

7. In *Emergence: The Connected Lives of Ants, Brains, Cities and Software,* author Steven Johnson does an excellent job of explaining this.

8. Christakis and Fowler, *Connected,* 24.

9. Ibid., 52.

10. Kuhn, *The Structure of Scientific Revolutions,* 158.

11. Branson, *Losing My Virginity,* 181; see also p. 451 of the expanded 2007 edition.

12. It's interesting to note that the average millionaire has a college GPA of about 2.92 (or a B-), and that includes millionaire physicians, who undoubtedly raise the average (this according to *The Millionaire Mind,* by Thomas Stanley [Kansas City, MO: Andrews McNeel Publishing, 2000]).

13. The wellspring for this can be found in *Emotional Intelligence: Key Readings on the Mayer and Salovey Model* by John Mayer, Peter Salovey et al.

14. Goleman, *Emotional Intelligence,* 221.

15. Damasio, *Descartes' Error,* 76, 121, 146.

16. LeDoux, *Synaptic Self,* 36. Damasio, *Descartes' Error,* 23.

17. This is described in Gazzaniga, *Human,* 104; also, Damasio, *Descartes' Error,* 135 and 141.

18. Myers, *Intuition,* 32.

19. Branson, *Losing My Virginity,* 115.

20. Hertzfeld, *Revolution in the Valley,* 76.

21. Amelio, *On the Firing Line,* 268.

22. Hertzfeld, *Revolution in the Valley,* 24.

23. Barrier, *The Animated Man,* 157.

24. Peri, *Working With Walt,* 7.

25. Gazzaniga, *Human,* 178.

26. See also Diane Mapes, "Loneliness Can Be Contagious," MSNBC .com, December 1, 2009.

27. Sculley, *Odyssey,* 131.

28. Peri, *Working With Walt,* 11. Ben Sharpsteen joined Disney in 1929. He was a key animator and director there until his death in 1980.

29. Goleman, *Emotional Intelligence,* 298.

30. Ibid., 78, 83.

31. Wilson, *Strangers to Ourselves,* 68.

32. Ibid., 72, 85.

33. Ibid., 84.

34. Goleman, *Emotional Intelligence,* 120.

35. Tolle, *A New Earth,* 107.

36. Peri, *Working With Walt,* 169.

37. Ibid., 138. Here Peri interviewed Ken Anderson, who started in 1934 with Disney as a director, and continued on as a key designer for Disneyland.

CHAPTER 7: Luck

1. Warner, *War Commentaries of Caesar,* 129.

2. Erik Calonius, "Their Wildest Dreams," *Fortune,* August 15, 1999.

3. Mlodinow, *The Drunkard's Walk,* 4, 11.

4. By Johanson, and collected in Richard Dawkins's *Oxford Book of Modern Science Writing,* 196.

5. Brian Arthur, "Positive Feedback in the Economy," *Scientific American,* February 1990, 92. Also see Mlodinow, *The Drunkard's Walk,* 204.

6. Taleb, *The Black Swan,* 105.

7. Woody Allen, *Without Feathers* (New York: Ballantine, 1986).

8. Mlodinow, *The Drunkard's Walk,* 187.

9. Erik Calonius, "Their Wildest Dreams," *Fortune,* August 15, 1999.

10. Raynoma Gordy Singleton, *Berry, Me and Motown,* 68. Berry Gordy's autobiography, *To Be Loved,* is, of course, a compelling look at the history of Motown.

11. Klein, *Secret Pulse of Time,* 231.

12. Huxley, *Knowledge, Morality and Destiny,* 16.

13. Kuhn, *The Structure of Scientific Revolutions,* 67.

14. Erik Calonius, "Their Wildest Dreams," *Fortune,* August 15, 1999.

15. Jakab, *Visions of a Flying Machine,* 17.

16. Huxley, *Knowledge, Morality and Destiny,* 71.

17. Wolpert, *Passionate Minds,* 200.

18. Barrier, *The Animated Man,* 5.

19. Mlodinow, *The Drunkard's Walk,* 217.

20. Softpedia, January 11, 2008 (pigs); *Biology News,* October 25, 2000 (bunny); *Harvard University Gazette,* March 9, 2006 (bunny and Leonardo's lizard).

21. "Green Fluorescent Pioneers Share Nobel Prize," *Science Daily,* October 8, 2008.

22. "Glowing Gene's Discoverer Left Out of Nobel Prize," National Public Radio, September 10, 2008; "Van Driver's Work in Massachusetts Aided Nobel Winners," Associated Press, October 11, 2008; "Genius Behind the Wheel," Inside Edition, National Public Radio, October 14, 2008.

23. "Local Biochemist Had Hand in Nobel," *Huntsville Times,* October 10, 2008; "Magical Nobel Trip Could Lead to New Opportunities," *Huntsville Times,* December 18, 2008.

CHAPTER 8: The Limits of Vision

1. In telling the story of Pixar, I am particularly indebted to David A. Price's *The Pixar Touch,* a marvelous narrative, and to Alan Deutschman's fascinating *The Second Coming of Steve Jobs.* I am also grateful for Karen Paik's history of Pixar in *To Infinity and Beyond.*

2. Lucas wanted $15 million in cash and $15 million in funding. Jobs countered with $5 million in cash and $5 million in funding. Paik, *To Infinity and Beyond,* 52.

3. For more on pattern making, see Taleb, *The Black Swan,* 65; Montague, *Your Brain Is (Almost) Perfect,* 67, 109; and Quartz, *Liars, Lovers and Heroes,* 101.

4. Pinker, *How the Mind Works,* 137. Also see Myers, *Intuition,* 54.

5. This is described by Lehrer in *How We Decide,* 25, and Burton's *On Being Certain,* 70.

6. Damasio, *Descartes' Error,* 165.

7. Dan Ariely explains this nicely in *Predictably Irrational,* 3.

8. See Daniel Kahneman, Amos Tversky, and Paul Slovic's seminal work, *Judgment Under Uncertainty.* For a detailed review of their work, see Mlodinow, *The Drunkard's Walk,* 7, and Gilovich, *How We Know What Isn't So,* 18. To better understand the "fast and frugal" rules of Kahneman and Tversky, see Dan Ariely's *Predictably Irrational; Gut Feelings* by Gigerenzer; and also Myers's *Intuition.*

9. Myers, *Intuition,* 121. Note that I've updated the numbers in this example. Also see Gilovich, *How We Know What Isn't So,* 18.

10. Myers, *Intuition,* 120.

11. Lynn Downey, *Levi Strauss & Co.* (San Francisco: Arcadia Publishing, 2007), 17. In *Strangers to Ourselves,* 30, Wilson notes how we are influenced by what came before, hence the power of an established brand.

12. "Police Arrest Prominent Black Historian for Breaking into His Own Home," Guardian.co.uk, July 21, 2009.

13. Ariely, *Predictably Irrational,* 23. See also Erik Calonius, "Tahitian Pearls," *Fortune,* December 20, 1999.

14. Kahneman, *Judgment Under Uncertainty,* 151.

15. Ibid., 14; also, Ariely, *Predictably Irrational,* 25.

16. Quartz, *Liars, Lovers and Heroes,* 41.

17. LeDoux, *Synaptic Self,* 251.

18. Anderson, Lepper, and Ross, "Perseverance of Social Theories," *Journal of Personality and Social Psychology,* 1980, vol. 39, no. 6.

19. Price, *The Pixar Touch,* 84.

20. Gilovich, *How We Know What Isn't So,* 86.

21. Myers, *Intuition,* 39.

22. See Ariely, *Predictably Irrational,* 134; also, Schwartz, *The Paradox of Choice,* 160.

23. Raymond S. Nickerson, "Confirmation Bias: A Ubiquitous Phenomenon in Many Guises," *Review of General Psychology,* vol. 2, no. 2 (1998), 175–220.

24. Charles G. Lord, Lee Ross, and Mark R. Lepper, "Biased Assimilation and Attitude Polarization," *Journal of Personality and Social Psychology,* vol. 37, no. 11 (1979), 2098–2109.

25. I've represented just part of the study here, and simplified it. For the full work (which is quite complex), see Drew Weston, Pavel Blagov, Keith Harenski, Clint Kilts, and Stephen Hamann, "Neural Bases of Motivated Reasoning," *Journal of Cognitive Neuroscience* 18:11 (2006), 1947–58.

26. Adamic and Glance, "The Political Blogospheres and the 2004 U.S. Election" (www.blogpulse.com/papers/2005/AdamicGlanceBlogwww.pdf). The image is reprinted in color and discussed as well in Christakis and Fowler's *Connected,* 206.

27. Sculley, *Odyssey,* 4.

28. Amelio, *On the Firing Line,* 281.

29. Price, *The Pixar Touch,* 142. See also Paik, *To Infinity and Beyond,* 80.

30. Deutschman, *The Second Coming of Steve Jobs,* 197.

31. Price, *The Pixar Touch,* 142.

32. Ibid., 154.

CHAPTER 9: When Genius Fails

1. In *The Fortune Sellers* (p. 69), William Sherden explains what complexity theory is, and why it fails as a long-range forecasting tool.

2. Ibid. Sherden describes the breadth of the industry (pp. 2–5).

3. See Werner DeBondt, "What Do Economists Know?" *Journal of Portfolio Management,* 85; also, Patric Andersson, "How Well Do Financial Experts Perform?" *SSE/EFI Working Paper Series in Business Administration,* no. 2004: 9, Center for Economic Psychology, Stockholm School of Economics, October 19, 2004.

4. Taleb, *The Black Swan,* 135.

5. Surowiecki, *The Wisdom of Crowds,* 33, quoting from John Bogle's *Bogle on Investing* (New York: McGraw-Hill, 2001), 21.

6. Sherden, *The Fortune Sellers,* 62, drawing on a study by Dr. Victor Zarnowitz, University of Chicago.

7. Louis Menand, "Everybody's an Expert," *New Yorker,* December 5, 2005. The study was conducted by University of California–Berkeley psychologist Philip Tetlock, who traced the predictions of 280 forecasters over 20 years. Tetlock's study is detailed in his book, *Expert Political Judgment: How Good Is It?* (Princeton: Princeton University Press, 2009).

8. "Garbage In, Garbage Out," *The Economist,* June 3, 1995.

9. See references in Malkiel, *A Random Walk Down Wall Street,* 15, 179.

10. See Georgette Jason, "Journal's Dartboard Retires," *Wall Street Journal,* April 18, 2002. See also, "Monkey Business," Google: Forbes,com,dartboard. Also, Jason Unger, automaticfinances.com/monkey-stock-picking/.

11. Taleb, *The Black Swan,* 135.

12. Sherden, *The Fortune Sellers,* 13.

13. Mlodinow, *The Drunkard's Walk,* 182.

14. See Quartz, *Liars, Lovers and Heroes,* 17, which draws on a study by Nissan and Bullemer, *Cognitive Pscyhology* 11:32 (1987); also see Aaron Kay et al., "Religious Belief as a Compensatory Control," *Personality and Social Psychology Review,* vol. 14, no. 1 (2000), 37.

15. Aaron Kay, *Journal of Personality and Social Psychology* 95, 18–35; also, J. A. Whitson, "Lacking Control Increases Illusory Pattern Perception," *Science* 322 (5898).

16. J. Scott Armstrong, "The Seersucker Theory," *Technology Review,* June 1980, 15.

17. Myers tells this story in *Intuition,* 136.

18. Ibid., 136. See also Gilovich, *How We Know What Isn't So,* 19, and Kahneman and Tversky, "Subjective Probability: A Judgment of Representatives," *Cognitive Pscyhology* 3(3), 430.

19. See David Braue at www.cnet.com.au/itunes-just-how-random-is-random, March 8, 2007.

20. Steven Levy, "Does Your iPod Play Favorites?" *Newsweek,* Technology and Science, November 28, 2009.

21. Gilovich, *How We Know What Isn't So,* 20.

22. Mlodinow, *The Drunkard's Walk,* 20.

23. Ibid., 177.

24. Tetlock, *Expert Political Judgment,* 61.

25. This experiment is detailed in Neisser and Winograd, *Affect and Accuracy in Recall: Studies of Flashbulb Memories* (New York: Cambridge University Press, 1992).

26. Full details are in Dan Offer et al., *Regular Guys: 34 Years Beyond Adolescence* (New York: Kluwer Academic Publishers, 2004).

27. Lehrer, *How We Decide,* 151, discusses the limitations of our memory.

28. Johnson, *Mind Wide Open,* 46, discusses how memories are formed.

29. Shah, *Cambridge Handbook,* 335.

30. Tavris and Aronson, *Mistakes Were Made,* 77. See also Tversky et al., "Spinning the Story of Our Lives," *Applied Cognitive Psychology* 18, 491.

31. Schwartz, *The Paradox of Choice,* 49.

32. Ibid., 52; also, Taleb, *The Black Swan,* 135.

33. See Tavris and Aronson, *Mistakes Were Made,* 77, citing a study by Barbara Tversky and Elizabeth Marsh, "Spinning the Stories of Our Lives," *Applied Cognitive Psychology* 18, 491. In the study, subjects were asked to read a story and then add their own details. What they remembered later was not the original story they read, but the details they added!

34. Daniel Schacter et al., "Remembering the Past to Imagine the Future," *Neuroscience,* vol. 8, September 2007, 657.

35. Sacks, *The Man Who Mistook His Wife for a Hat,* 13.

36. Klein, *Secret Pulse of Time,* 102; also, Thomas Suddendorf, "Mental Time Travel and the Shaping of the Human Mind," *Psychological Transactions of the Royal Society,* B2009364, 1317. This experiment is described in Demis Hassabis et al., "Patients with Hippocampus Amnesia Cannot Imagine New Experiences," Wellcome Trust Center for Neuroimaging, 2007.

37. Daniel Schacter, "Remembering the Past to Imagine the Future," *Neuroscience,* vol. 8, September 2007, 675.

38. See Charles McGrath's review of "Genius in Disguise: Harold Ross of the New Yorker," *New Yorker,* February 20, 1995.

39. Saul Steinberg, "View of the World from Ninth Avenue," *New Yorker,* March 29, 1976.

40. Cecil Adams, "Does the Average American Student Have Less Vocabulary Today Than in Days Gone By?" www.straightdope.com/columns/read/2724/, September 7, 2007.

41. Taleb, *The Black Swan,* 283.

42. Erik Calonius, "Stiff Upper Lips Get a Bit More Relaxed on the First of April," *Wall Street Journal,* March 30, 1984, 1.

43. Roger Harrabin, "Climate Prediction: No Model for Success," BBC News, November 25, 2009.

44. For a fearless critique of computer forecasting, see Orrin Pilkey and Linda Pilkey-Jarvis's *Useless Arithmetic,* 33.

45. This cartoon is reprinted on p. 38 of Dennett's *Consciousness Explained.*

46. Pilkey, *Useless Arithmetic,* 36.

47. Ibid., 39.

48. James O'Malley, "From Science to Illusion: Mathematics in Fishing Management," International Ocean Institute. See also www.fishingnj.org.artomalley.htm.

49. Taleb, *The Black Swan*, 44.

50. Branson, *Losing My Virginity*, 345.

CHAPTER 10: Can You Learn Vision?

1. "Who Needs NASA?" *Wired* 8.01, January 2000.

2. Belfiore, *Rocketeers: How a Visionary Band of Business Leaders, Engineers, and Pilots Is Boldly Privatizing Space*, 102. Also, Sam Verhovek, "Space Inc.," *Popular Science*, January 2010.

3. Pinker, *How the Mind Works*, 361.

4. Quartz, *Liars, Lovers and Heroes*, 27.

5. Eric Kandel, *In Search of Memory*, 145, 204. To see fascinating interviews with Kandel, go to www.news/columbia.edu/oncampus/1787 and www.kavlifoundation.org/eric-kandel.

6. Kandel, *In Search of Memory*, 275.

7. Quartz, *Liars, Lovers and Heroes*, 44; and LeDoux, *Synaptic Self*, 9.

8. For more on the Rosensteil *aplysia* project, see www.aplysia.miami.edu/.

9. Bernstein, *Sparks of Genius*, 63.

10. Groopman, *How Doctors Think*, 20.

11. Harper Lee, *To Kill a Mockingbird*, 30.

12. Mlodinow, *The Drunkard's Walk*, 217.

13. Richard Wiseman, "Be Lucky: It's an Easy Skill to Learn," www.telegraph.co.uk/technology/3304496/Be-lucky-its-an-easy-skill. Also, see his book, *The Luck Factor* (New York: Miramax Books Hyperion, 2003).

14. This is described in Gigerenzer, *Gut Feelings*, 9. Such feedback loops are also discussed in Judson, *Search for Solutions*, 104–12.

15. Gabler, *Walt Disney*, 87.

16. Taleb, *The Black Swan*, 222.

17. Tolle, *A New Earth*, 108.

18. Details drawn from Murry Keith, "A Q&A with Fred Woodward," *Memphis*, April 1, 2006; see also Art Directors Hall of Fame profile, and liner notes from CD collection *Jack's Darkroom Music*.

BIBLIOGRAPHY

Amelio, Gil. *On the Firing Line.* New York: Harper Business, 1998.

Ariely, Dan. *Predictably Irrational.* New York: HarperCollins, 2008.

Arp, Robert. *Scenario Visualization.* Cambridge, MA: MIT Press, 2008.

Barabasi, Albert-Laszlo. *Linked.* New York: Plume Books, 2003.

Barrier, Michael. *The Animated Man.* Los Angeles: University of California Press, 2007.

Belfiore, Michael. *Rocketeers.* New York: HarperCollins, 2008.

Berns, Gregory. *Iconoclast.* Boston: Harvard Business School Press, 2008.

Bernstein, Robert, and Michele Bernstein. *Sparks of Genius.* New York: Houghton Mifflin, 1999.

Best, Joel. *Damned Lies and Statistics.* Los Angeles: University of California Press, 2001.

Branson, Richard. *Losing My Virginity.* London: Virgin Books, 2004; expanded edition, 2007.

Burton, Robert. *On Being Certain.* New York: St. Martin's Griffin, 2008.

Butter, Andrea, and David Pogue. *Piloting Palm.* New York: John Wiley, 2002.

Chabris, Christopher, and Daniel Simons. *The Invisible Gorilla.* New York: Crown, 2010.

Christakis, Nicholas, and James Fowler. *Connected.* New York: Little, Brown, 2009.

Damasio, Antonio. *Descartes' Error.* New York: Penguin Books, 1994.

———. *The Feeling of What Happens.* New York: Harvest Books, 1999.

———. *Looking for Spinoza.* New York: Harvest Books, 2003.

Dawkins, Richard. *Oxford Book of Modern Science Writing.* Oxford: Oxford University Press, 2008.

De Kruif, Paul. *Microbe Hunters.* New York: Harvest Books, 1996.

Dennett, Daniel. *Consciousness Explained.* New York: Back Bay Books, 1991.

———. *Darwin's Dangerous Idea.* New York: Simon and Schuster, 1995.

Deutschman, Alan. *The Second Coming of Steve Jobs.* New York: Broadway Books, 2001.

Doidge, Norman. *The Brain That Changes Itself.* New York: Penguin Books, 2007.

Ferguson, Eugene. *Engineering and the Mind's Eye.* Cambridge, MA: MIT Press, 1999.

Feynman, Richard. *Surely You're Joking, Mr. Feynman!* New York: W. W. Norton, 1985.

Gabler, Neal. *Walt Disney: Triumph of American Imagination.* New York: Alfred A. Knopf, 2006.

Galton, Francis. *Inquiries into Human Faculty and Understanding.* London: J. M. Dent, 1907.

Gazzaniga, Michael. *Human.* New York: HarperCollins, 2008.

Gigerenzer, Gerd. *Gut Feelings.* New York: Viking Press, 2007.

Gilovich, Thomas. *How We Know What Isn't So.* New York: Free Press, 1991.

Gladwell, Malcolm. *Blink.* New York: Back Bay Books, 2005.

———. *The Tipping Point.* New York: Little, Brown, 2007.

Goldberg, Elkhonon. *The Wisdom Paradox.* New York: Gotham Books, 2005.

Goleman, Daniel. *Emotional Intelligence.* New York: Bantam Books, 1997.

Gordy, Berry. *To Be Loved.* New York: Warner Books, 1994.

Gould, Stephen Jay. *Full House.* New York: Three Rivers Press, 1996.

Grafen, Alan, and Mark Ridley. *Richard Dawkins.* New York: Oxford University Press, 2006.

Groopman, Jerome. *How Doctors Think.* New York: Mariner Books, 2008.

Grove, Andrew. *Only the Paranoid Survive.* New York: Currency, 1999.

Hanson, Norwood. *Perception and Discovery.* San Francisco: Freeman, Cooper, 1969.

Hawkins, Jeff. *On Intelligence.* New York: Times Books, 2004.

Hertzfeld, Andy. *Revolution in the Valley.* Sebastopol, CA: O'Reilly Media, 2005.

Hogan, James. *Mind Matters.* New York: Ballantine, 1997.

Hogarth, Robin. *Educating Intuition.* Chicago: University of Chicago Press, 2001.

Hunter, Ian. *Memory.* London: Penguin Books, 1964.

Hurlburt, Russell. *Describing Inner Experience.* Cambridge, MA: MIT Press, 2007.

Huxley, Julian. *Knowledge, Morality and Destiny.* New York: Harper and Brothers, 1957.

Jackson, Tim. *Inside Intel*. New York: Plume Books, 1997.

Jakab, Peter. *Visions of a Flying Machine*. Washington, DC: Smithsonian Institution Press, 1990.

Johnson, Steven. *Emergence*. New York: Scribner, 2001.

———. *Mind Wide Open*. New York: Scribner, 2004.

Judson, Horace. *The Search for Solutions*. Baltimore: Johns Hopkins University Press, 1987.

Kahneman, Daniel, Amos Tversky, and Paul Slovic. *Judgment Under Uncertainty*. New York: Cambridge University Press, 1982.

Kahney, Leander. *Inside Steve's Brain*. New York: Portfolio, 2008.

Kandel, Eric. *In Search of Memory*. New York: W. W. Norton, 2006.

Klein, Stefan. *The Science of Happiness*. New York: Da Capo Press, 2006.

———. *Secret Pulse of Time*. New York: Da Capo Press, 2007.

Koch, Christof. *The Quest for Consciousness*. Englewood, CO: Roberts, 2004.

Kosslyn, Stephen, and Oliver Koenig. *Wet Minds*. New York: Free Press, 1995.

Kuhn, Thomas. *The Structure of Scientific Revolutions*. Chicago: University of Chicago Press, 1962.

LeDoux, Joseph. *Synaptic Self*. New York: Viking Penguin, 2002.

Lee, Harper. *To Kill a Mockingbird*. New York: Warner Books, 1960.

Le Fanu, James. *The Rise and Fall of Modern Medicine*. New York: Carroll and Graf, 1999.

Lehrer, Jonah. *How We Decide*. New York: Houghton Mifflin Harcourt, 2009.

Levitin, Daniel. *This Is Your Brain on Music*. New York: Plume Books, 2006.

Lowenstein, Roger. *When Genius Failed*. New York: Random House, 2000.

Malkiel, Burton. *A Random Walk Down Wall Street*. New York: W. W. Norton, 2007.

Mamet, David. *Glengarry Glen Ross*. New York: Grove Press, 1982.

Mayer, John, Peter Salovey, et al. *Emotional Intelligence: Key Readings*. Port Chester, NY: Dude Publishing, 2007.

McKenzie, A. E. E. *The Major Achievements of Science*. New York: Touchstone, 1973.

Mlodinow, Leonard. *The Drunkard's Walk*. New York: Vintage Books, 2009.

Montague, Read. *Your Brain Is (Almost) Perfect*. New York: Plume Books, 2007.

Myers, David. *Intuition*. New Haven: Yale University Press, 2002.

Newberg, Andrew, and Mark Waldman. *Why We Believe What We Believe*. New York: Free Press, 2006.

Noe, Alva. *Out of Our Heads*. New York: Hill and Wang, 2009.

Offer, Daniel, Marjorie Offer, and Eric Ostrov. *Regular Guys*. New York: Kluwer Academic Publishing, 2004.

Paik, Karen. *To Infinity and Beyond.* San Francisco: Chronicle Books, 2007.

Peri, Don. *Working With Walt.* Jackson: University of Mississippi Press, 2008.

Piattelli-Palmarini, Massimo. *Inevitable Illusions.* New York: John Wiley, 1994.

Pilkey, Orrin, and Linda Pilkey-Jarvis. *Useless Arithmetic.* New York: Columbia University Press, 2007.

Pinker, Steven. *How the Mind Works.* New York: W. W. Norton, 1997.

Polykoff, Shirley. *Does She or Doesn't She?* New York: Doubleday, 1975.

Price, David. *The Pixar Touch.* New York: Vintage Books, 2008.

Quartz, Steven, and Terrence Sejnowski. *Liars, Lovers, and Heroes.* New York: HarperCollins, 2002.

Quirk, Mark. *Intuition and Metacognition in Medical Education.* New York: Springer Publishing, 2006.

Rollo, Vera. *Burt Rutan: Reinventing the Airplane.* Lanham: Maryland Historic Press, 1991.

Sacks, Oliver. *The Man Who Mistook His Wife for a Hat.* New York: Perennial Books, 1987.

Schacter, Daniel. *Searching for Memory.* New York: Basic Books, 1996.

————. *The Seven Sins of Memory.* New York: Houghton Mifflin, 2001.

Schickel, Richard. *The Disney Version.* Chicago: Elephant Paperbacks, 1997.

Schwartz, Barry. *The Paradox of Choice.* New York: HarperCollins, 2005.

Sculley, John. *Odyssey.* New York: Perennial Books, 1987.

Shah, Priti, and Akira Miyake. *Cambridge Handbook of Visuospatial Thinking.* New York: Cambridge University Press, 2005.

Sherden, William. *The Fortune Sellers.* New York: John Wiley, 1998.

Shubin, Neil. *Your Inner Fish.* New York: Vintage Press, 2008.

Singleton, Raynoma. *Berry, Me, and Motown.* Chicago: Contemporary Books, 1990.

Stibel, Jeffrey. *Wired for Thought.* Boston: Harvard Business School Press, 2009.

Surowiecki, James. *The Wisdom of Crowds.* New York: Anchor Books, 2005.

Taleb, Nassim. *The Black Swan.* New York: Random House, 2007.

Taubes, Gary. *Nobel Dreams.* Redmond, WA: Tempus Books, 1986.

Tavris, Carol, and Elliot Aronson. *Mistakes Were Made.* New York: Harvest Books, 2007.

Tedlow, Richard. *Andy Grove.* New York: Portfolio, 2006.

Tetlock, Philip. *Expert Political Judgment.* Princeton: Princeton University Press, 2005.

Thomas, Bob. *An American Original: Walt Disney.* New York: Disney Editions, 1994.

Tolle, Eckhart. *A New Earth.* New York: Plume Books, 2006.

Von Furstenberg, Diane. *Diane: A Signature Life.* New York: Simon and Schuster, 1998.

Warner, Rex. *War Commentaries of Caesar.* New York: Mentor Books, 1963.

Wilson, Timothy. *Strangers to Ourselves.* Cambridge, MA: Harvard University Press, 2002.

Wolpert, Lewis, and Alison Richards. *Passionate Minds.* Oxford: Oxford University Press, 1997.

Wozniak, Steve. *iWoz.* New York: W. W. Norton, 2006.

Young, Jeffrey, and William Simon. *iCon: Steve Jobs.* New York: John Wiley, 2005.

Zimmer, Carl. *Soul Made Flesh.* New York: Free Press, 2004.

INDEX